THE BOSTON

PARANORMAL ARCHIVES

BARRY CORBETT

FONTHILL

For Tom Elliott, my friend and mentor.
Godspeed, Tom.

Fonthill Media Inc.
www.fonthill.media
office@fonthillmedia.com

First published 2024
Copyright © Barry Corbett 2024

ISBN 978-1-62545-141-5

Typeset in Sabon
Printed and bound in England

CONTENTS

INTRODUCTION

Boston Paranormal Investigators was founded by our president, Tom Elliott, in 2005. We are one of the longest-running investigative groups in the Boston area. Our members come from varying backgrounds, but they all have one thing in common: a burning desire to explore the fascinating mysteries that our world has to offer. Foremost, in my opinion, is the topic of ghosts. No matter how thoroughly we research and analyze paranormal phenomena, we are often left with more questions than answers. Deceased spirits interact with psychics and mediums on a regular basis, but those of us who do not have their unique gifts can only rely on observable phenomena.

I discovered Boston Paranormal through MeetUp and joined in February 2017. Tom had run the group for fourteen years, but his health began to deteriorate, and he handed me the reins. I had only minimal experience with the paranormal but have been obsessed with death since early childhood when, only a few days before his eighth birthday, a ruptured appendix took the life of my older brother, Grafton. As you can imagine, this horrific tragedy left my parents in a state of complete shock. No matter how they tried to explain it to me, I just could not wrap my head around it. Is he in Heaven? Can he see us? Will I ever see him again? These questions were never answered to my satisfaction, and here I am, decades later, still trying to sort it out.

Can consciousness exist beyond the point of death? If discarnate spirits maintain their identities, their memories, and personalities beyond the dissolution of their bodies, does that not prove the existence of the soul? These are existential issues, debated by writers, poets, philosophers, and theologians since the dawn of humankind.

What lies beyond the veil? We can only speculate, but I have seen enough physical evidence to convince me that ghosts do walk among us. This book is my opportunity to share some of our most memorable experiences from the past six years of paranormal investigating. The New England area is a treasure trove of historical lore, and you will find that many of the stories and locations that I have chosen are linked to seminal events in American history.

Before we dive in, I should give you a brief description of our investigative process and describe some of the tools we utilize. With any haunted site, our goal is simple: determine if the reported phenomena can be explained by natural causes or is paranormal in nature.

Historical research is a large part of it. Whether we are handling a private case or conducting a public investigation, the first step is to gather as much information as possible. The local library is an excellent source for town history, and the Registry of Deeds has an online repository of mortgages, deeds, engineering plans, and real estate transactions. Census records available through genealogical websites can tell us who lived at a chosen location within certain time periods, and we can access digital libraries for historical maps, which often indicate the names of property owners. Having armed ourselves with some advanced scouting, we can now direct our line of questioning as appropriate.

Next, we look at environmental factors, areas where faulty wiring, Wi-Fi routers, power supplies, or appliances might emit a random electrical surge. An extremely high electromagnetic field can cause headaches, dizziness, and hallucinations. Carbon dioxide, radon gas, and excessive mold can also be factors. Once we have ruled out these external forces, we can turn our attention to ghosts.

EVP SESSION

Better known as electronic voice phenomenon, the use of audio recorders has supplied us with more evidence than any other tool. Ghost hunting is a game for the patient. We often spend hours sitting in darkened rooms, asking questions, and hoping that spirits are in the mood to communicate. During an investigation, we may hear nothing more than our own voices, but when we analyze the recordings, we sometimes find that a ghostly response has been imprinted on the digital file. There are three categories for EVPs, defined by their clarity:

Class A: A clear and distinct voice that everybody can understand without headphones or enhancement.

Class B: A voice that is loud and distinct but subject to interpretation. It can be heard without the use of headphones. Music, footsteps, or knocking sounds fall under Class B.

Class C: A faint or indistinct voice that is barely heard and difficult to decipher. Headphones are necessary and there is no consensus on what was said.

K-II AND MEL-METER

Every location displays different levels of electromagnetic radiation. We use EMF meters to detect anomalies and measure the strength of the electromagnetic field. Ghosts are believed to generate a certain level of electrical activity. When we see a spike in EMF (measured in milligauss), we know that something out of the ordinary has affected the environment.

REM POD

REM is shorthand for radiating electromagnetic, since the REM Pod generates its own small, magnetic field. When a human body or, theoretically, a noncorporeal entity gets close enough to interact with the field, it lights up and sounds an alert.

INFRARED PHOTOGRAPHY

The human eye perceives images within a narrow spectrum of radiation referred to as visible light. Custom-made cameras can capture images in different wavelengths. Infrared radiation has a longer wavelength than visible light, while ultraviolet radiation has a shorter wavelength. Thus, infrared is used by the military to see combatants in the dark and by ghost hunters to detect entities unseen by the human eye.

SPIRIT BOX

The SB-7 Spirit Box is a frequency sweeper. Like a radio with a moving dial, it sweeps up and down the frequencies too quickly for a radio station to broadcast more than a single word. While sweeping along, it generates white noise. Very often entire sentences are captured, whereas a radio station would be quickly cut off as the Spirit Box passes on to the next frequency.

ESTES METHOD

Invented at Estes Park in Colorado, the site of the famously haunted Stanley Hotel, it is a variation on the Spirit Box session. The sitter uses a blindfold and noise-canceling headphones while listening to the SB-7 sweep through radio frequencies. Because they cannot hear the questions being asked, it is highly unlikely that the sitter will be able to answer in a corresponding fashion. If their answers line up with the questions, then perhaps they are coming from an outside source, presumably a spirit.

THERMAL IMAGING CAMERA

FLIR is an acronym for forward-looking infrared. The camera projects an infrared beam designed to measure the temperature of the selected surface. A graphics program then maps out an image, based on generated heat. Living creatures will show up in the warmer colors—red, orange, and yellow. Theoretically, a spirit trying to manifest will use up the energy within the room and cause the surrounding temperature to drop. Said phantom should show up in the cooler tints—mostly green and blue.

STATIC FIELD METER

Static electricity is created by friction. Instead of flowing along a circuit, the electrons in an object build up, then they move from one object to another, creating a charge imbalance when the two separate. The static field meter lights up when a static charge is detected.

MOTION DETECTORS

We usually leave a few of these in unoccupied rooms. They emit ultrasonic sound waves that reflect off moving objects and sound an alert. It helps us determine where to focus our attention.

Of course, they are always coming up with new products. If there is one thing that ghost hunters love, it is a new gadget! Now that we have described some of our tools, let us move on to the locations that BPI has explored. This collection offers unique areas with New England historical connections. I am constantly amazed by the unusual stories that come to light as we learn about these haunted sites. I hope that you will get the same thrill that we experienced as you enjoy this sampling of tales from the Boston Paranormal archives.

1

BURIED ALIVE AT DUNGEON ROCK

Concealed within the Lynn Woods Reservation, there lies a hidden gem. Barely visible alongside a well-traveled hiking path, tucked inside a crevice between two giant rock formations, there is a rusted, steel door that leads into a darkened cave. A 20-foot ladder descends into complete darkness, where an excavated passageway extends beyond the chamber, twisting and turning for 150 feet, where it finally ends in a stagnant pool of water. Somewhere down in that cave lie the remains of the infamous pirate Thomas Veale, who spent the final years of his life hiding within its confines.

Dungeon Rock stands at the apex of Pirate's Glen. The earthquake split the rock formation in two and entombed Captain Veale within his cave.

The story began in 1654, when residents spied an unmarked ship anchored in Lynn Harbor. As it flew no identifying colors, they believed it to be a pirate vessel and kept it under close observation. They saw a smaller boat lowered over the side of the ship and watched four men load a large container aboard, then row up the Saugus River and out of sight. The pirate ship set sail without them.

A few days later, they found an anonymous note posted at the nearby Saugus Iron Works, requesting a list of specific supplies. In return for some custom-made digging tools, shackles, chains, and hatchets, the pirates offered them a generous quantity of silver. The townsfolk decided to fill the order, so they met with the four privateers at a predetermined site and completed the transaction. This area was chosen for its elevation, which afforded them a clear view of the harbor and the surrounding woods. In later years, it came to be known as Pirate's Glen.

Nothing was heard from the pirates for a few months. During that time, word got around that they had used the tools to bury their ill-gotten plunder somewhere within the reservation. The four men returned a year later, one of them bearing a young bride at his side. They settled near Pirate's Glen, built a few makeshift cabins, planted crops, and dug a well. Within just a few months, the woman contracted smallpox and died.

Piracy was at its peak in the 1650s. Captain Thomas Veale and his crew were ransacking ships along the New England coastline. When a rumor about Pirate's Glen reached their ears, the British quickly sent a ship, raised a small militia from the townsfolk, and searched the woods. They captured three of the pirates, but Veale escaped into the forest. The three prisoners were brought to England, tried, convicted, and hanged, but the British authorities never located Veale.

Captain Veale had hidden within the cave, dug himself a cozy little niche, and managed to survive there for years. The townsfolk were well aware of his identity, but having no love for the British, they never revealed his location. Periodically, he came into the village to trade for food and materials, and he took on contract work as a shoemaker.

In February 1663, a massive earthquake struck the area, causing the cave's entrance to collapse. Thomas Veale was entombed within his chamber, never to be seen again. For 200 years, the site lay untouched, but rumors of that hidden stash continued to entice treasure seekers.

In 1829, Alonzo Lewis dedicated a chapter to Veale's treasure in his treatise *The History of Lynn*, renewing public interest in the legend. In the 1830s, Lynn residents made two unsuccessful attempts to reopen the cave by igniting kegs full of gunpowder, which resulted in the complete destruction of the original entrance.

Here, the story takes a bizarre turn. Charlestown native Hiram Marble purchased 5 acres of the land surrounding Dungeon Rock from the City of Lynn. Marble, a member of the rapidly growing Spiritualistic Church, was convinced that he could communicate with the ghost of Thomas Veale, and with the dead pirate's assistance, he would locate the treasure. He built several long-term structures at the site, including a two-story house for his wife and son, a tool shed, a blast wall, and a guest house.

Marble doggedly excavated the passageway by day, and by night he would attempt to communicate with Thomas Veale. He consulted with mediums who used a form of channeling called automatic writing, in which they enter a trance-like state, allowing spirits to control their bodies and transcribe their messages. They also conducted candlelit séances, during which they received specific details on where to dig.

Marble originally planned to dig a new tunnel beside Veale's chamber and, when they got beyond the collapsed entrance, they would turn to the left and connect with the original cave. But he received conflicting messages from the entities. They instructed him to change the tunnel's direction several times, as they chipped and blasted their way almost 150 feet beyond the new entrance. It was a dangerous and laborious undertaking. Hiram carefully drilled tiny holes into the rock face, filling them with gunpowder. Then, he lit the fuse and ran for cover. Once the blast had done its work, he removed the dirt and granite in wicker baskets, dumping it outside the entrance. This went on for decades at the snail's pace of 5 feet per year. They found no sign of Veale's body, nor his treasure.

In the end, Marble and his son, Edwin, spent thirty years digging out the passageway, while his fortune dwindled. Finally, in a desperate plan to raise money, he turned the cave into a tourist attraction, charging visitors a quarter for the pleasure of exploring the famous pirate's hideout. Marble also enticed investors to purchase bonds with the promise they would receive a full share of the treasure.

Hiram Marble died in 1868, but Edwin continued the search for Veale's treasure until his own death in 1880. Hiram is interred at Bay Path Cemetery in Charlestown. Edwin left instructions to bury him at the site of Dungeon Rock. To the left of the entrance, his gravesite is marked by a large, pink boulder. None of Marble's buildings remain, but the pathway leading up to Dungeon Rock is still covered in the gravel they removed from the interior over a thirty-year period.

A 20-foot ladder descends into complete darkness.

These events coincided with the growing spiritualist movement created by the Fox sisters in Upstate New York. What began as eerie knocking sounds inside their home resulted in a wave of national media attention when the two sisters claimed to communicate with the spirits of the dead. Hiram Marble was a strong believer in this practice.

In my research, I uncovered a book published by Hiram in 1859 entitled *The History of Dungeon Rock*, in which he relays a fantastic tale conveyed to him by a medium, Madame Lamphier. Through automatic writing, she dictated the details given to her by the spirit of Captain Veale. In her version, Veale arrived in the company of Captain Harris, and it was Harris who arranged the trade with the Iron Works. When the two men returned a year later, Harris brought his bride, Cathryn, and they eventually had a daughter, Arabel. The child died and was buried near Pirate's Glen. Harris then sailed back to England on some mission, leaving Cathryn at Dungeon Rock with Veale. Harris never returned, and Cathryn contracted smallpox, passed away, and was buried within the cave. The earthquake struck shortly afterward and entombed Thomas Veale. Hiram wrote that a different medium, Madame Emerson, told him to locate the pirate's tomb, and that he would eventually discover the treasure. She predicted that Marble would quickly find an artifact that would prove the existence of Thomas Veale. Less than a month after working on the tunnel, Hiram unearthed a rusty sword and brass scabbard belonging to Captain Veale, which he later displayed for visitors.

As a paranormal investigator, I have experienced a wide range of phenomena. We generally divide spirits into four categories: intelligent ghosts, residual ghosts, poltergeists, and elementals. The elementals can be aggressive. Various cultures and religions refer to them as jinns, fairies, poltergeists, Pukwudgies, and demons. The spiritualists believe they are negative entities, evil spirits that have never walked upon this Earth. They exist in a lower dimension but thrive on the energy they create by introducing chaos into our physical plane. I have read countless stories about spirits reaching out through the Ouija board, a séance, or some other form of channeling, all the while pretending to be the spirit of a loved one who has crossed over. They tell the sitter what they want to hear and gradually gain their trust. Then they dole out advice that is counter to the sitter's best interests, often with catastrophic results. The chaos that ensues supplies them with life-sustaining energy, while destroying the lives of their misguided followers.

This may be what Hiram Marble encountered while seeking the spirit of Thomas Veale. Could one of these negative entities have seen an opportunity to send Marble and his son on a thirty-year wild goose chase? It might explain his curious decision to divert the new tunnel away from the spot where Veale's cave collapsed.

On the morning of January 6, 2021, we set out to investigate Dungeon Rock. The day was overcast, with a slight breeze, so we made sure to cover our digital recorders with wind screens. They are designed to reduce whistling sounds, but they are never completely eliminated. We chose four different spots to conduct our EVP sessions: the entrance to the cave, an outcropping above the cleft, the foundation of Marble's home, and the pink boulder marking Edwin Marble's gravesite. The tunnel itself was closed during the pandemic, but we later returned to explore the passageway.

Michelle Ross joined me, an experienced investigator who describes herself as a sensitive, somebody who reacts to physical sensations in the presence of phenomena. In the past, I have experienced dizzy spells, sudden headaches, electrical charges, and subtle vibrations at haunted locations, but would not describe myself as overly

The 150-foot tunnel takes numerous turns and descends well below Veale's original cave.

sensitive. I believe there are varying levels of sensitivity, and Michelle is much more in tune with her environment.

At the peak of the cleft, Michelle got a severe dizzy spell, strong enough to force her to sit down until it passed. We had chosen this spot because it was above Veale's original cave entrance. We stayed about thirty minutes, asking questions while recording audio for later review. It is not uncommon for a response that was never heard at the time to later appear on the audio file.

We moved down to the steel door at the entrance to Marble's tunnel and set up the Spirit Box SB-7 for a session. The Spirit Box sweeps through radio frequencies, traveling up and down the AM or FM dial at preset rates. We are trying to use the white noise in-between frequencies to allow spirits to communicate. In past sessions, we have heard complete sentences come through, which is unlikely to be confused with a radio broadcast. We had the sweep rate set up for 150 milliseconds. At this speed, even if a radio station were to bleed over from one frequency to the next, it should sweep on by too quickly for more than a single word to come from one of the hosts. Only two words came across clearly: "Erick" and "Eleven." Interestingly, the Mel-Meter spiked a couple of times, registering 1.2 mG and 1.5 mG. We wondered if the Lynn Park Rangers had strung some electrical lighting inside the locked chamber, but that seemed unlikely, since the cave was more than a mile from the surrounding town. Our return trip confirmed that there was no electricity within the tunnel, so the Mel-Meter should have registered as zero.

A steel door conceals the entrance to Hiram Marble's tunnel.

Next, we moved down to the boulder marking Edwin's grave and conducted another EVP session. Upon playback, we heard a low moan, like something out of a horror movie, but that could easily have been an artifact caused by the wind. We explored the remnants of Edwin's foundation and conducted EVP sessions in two more areas, but that was it for evidence. We hiked nearly a mile back to our cars and went our separate ways.

In July 2023, Michelle and I returned to Dungeon Rock, since the cave was once again open to the public. We walked through the steel door, climbed down the 20-foot ladder, and stepped into a dark chamber. The granite surface was damp, slippery, and uneven, with water constantly dripping from the ceiling of the cavern. Carrying a lantern, a Mel-Meter, and three recorders, we ventured into the tunnel. The light from the entrance disappeared as we rounded the first turn, and the passageway descended into pitch darkness. By the time we reached the tunnel's end, it had turned and twisted numerous times, and we had to crouch to avoid hitting the ceiling. We settled down at its lowest point, turned on our recorders, and, for the next hour, attempted to communicate with Captain Veale. The EMF reading never went above zero, and the only sound we heard was the incessant dripping. Either Veale was not down here, or he was not in the mood for conversation.

We decided to conduct one more session near the base of the ladder, since that was the closest point to Veale's original cave. At one point, we thought we heard a voice, but the dripping water created echoes that reverberated throughout the cavern. We remained for thirty more minutes, then packed our gear and climbed up out of the darkness. At the area near Hiram's grave, we conducted a Spirit Box session, but nothing really stood out, so we called it a day and returned home.

The path to Dungeon Rock is strewn with gravel that Hiram Marble removed from his tunnel.

When we reviewed our audio files, we realized that the last session in the cavern had produced two intriguing EVPs. In answer to Michelle's question, "Captain Veale, were you trapped inside this cavern?" we heard a very clear, "Yes." Four minutes later, we caught a male voice, but it was difficult to make out the words. I had mentioned that Veale's three shipmates had been captured and brought to trial, and in response I felt the voice had whispered, "Hanged." Michelle thought the spirit was repeating my own words back to me. It is very common for each person to hear different words in the same EVP. When analyzing a Class B category EVP, we have to consider confirmation bias, the tendency for people to subconsciously seek out information that is consistent with their existing beliefs. In simpler terms, they hear what they want to hear. It is similar to pareidolia, the ability to pick out familiar patterns in random visual information. For example, an image reflected in a window displays an indistinct shape, but we might perceive it as a human face.

When researching this case, I had originally believed the pirate tale was just an urban legend. There is no way to know if Captain Veale died within his cavern or had the good fortune to be out in the forest when the earthquake struck. It is just as likely that he had moved away, long before the cave entrance collapsed, or perhaps the entire story was fiction. There was no physical proof, just word of mouth handed down for 350 years.

At least, I felt that way until I heard the EVP near the tunnel entrance. Now, I am not so sure. We will certainly return to investigate Dungeon Rock, but for now, it is another mystery for the archives.

Edwin Marble's gravesite is marked by a giant boulder.

Hiram Marble's advertisement appeared in Frank Leslie's *Illustrated Newspaper* in 1878.

2

OLIVER HOUSE AND THE SONS OF LIBERTY

The Peter Oliver House is reputed to be one of the most haunted buildings in New England. For me, it holds a special significance as it was the site of my first public investigation with the paranormal group and continues to be my favorite. On a warm, summer evening in August 2017, we visited the Oliver Estate for a five-hour investigation. This Georgian-style mansion, built in 1769, features eight fireplaces, a carriage house, a two-story barn, an English garden maze, two hidden chambers, and a secret tunnel.

Oliver House is one of two buildings constructed at the site by the well-respected Judge Peter Oliver, a graduate of Harvard University and one of the richest men in Middleborough. A staunch Loyalist to the king of England, he supported the unpopular notion that the colonists should be taxed. Governor Thomas Hutchinson shared that view and appointed Peter as Chief Justice of the Massachusetts Superior Court in 1756. Judge Oliver was one of three judges on the bench for the famous Boston Massacre Trial, when eight British soldiers were tried for murder in 1770. John Adams served as a lawyer for the defense.

But things were stirring in Boston, and those who remained loyal to the king found themselves the object of great hostility. Judge Oliver was impeached in 1774 for accepting a salary from the crown and refusing to forswear his allegiance to England.

For eleven years, Judge Oliver had been operating an iron forge on the banks of the Nemasket River, where he manufactured cannons, mortar, and shells. The ironworks turned a huge profit, and he used his wealth to construct two gentry mansions nearby, the Georgian-style Peter Oliver House and the ostentatious Oliver Hall, where he hosted grand parties and entertained luminaries loyal to the king. In 1770, Judge Oliver's son, Peter, married Sally Hutchinson, youngest daughter of the governor. The Peter Oliver House was built as a wedding gift for the young couple.

The Oliver family enjoyed a privileged lifestyle, and they employed a group of gardeners, chambermaids, and caretakers who were not always well treated. One of the laborers was involved in a violent altercation with Peter Oliver over his treatment of Julie, one of the chambermaids. Peter had the man dragged out to the back yard and executed, his body left hanging from a tree limb for a full week. This cruel action led to serious repercussions.

Peter Oliver House, a Georgian-style mansion, was constructed in 1769.

While cleaning in Peter's bedroom, Julie discovered a packet of written correspondence between Judge Oliver and Loyalist Thomas Whately. Whately was a member of the British parliament who supported the Stamp Act of 1765, generally considered the match that ignited the American Revolution. Julie saw an opportunity to strike back at Peter Oliver, and she used her local connections to send word to the Sons of Liberty in Boston. A few weeks later, Benjamin Franklin was invited to one of Judge Oliver's lavish dinner parties. He accepted the invitation, hoping to secure this damning evidence of Peter's British loyalties. During the evening, Franklin convinced Judge Oliver and Governor Hutchinson to leave Oliver Hall and hold a quiet meeting at Peter's home. Somehow, Julie managed to get the letters into the hands of Ben Franklin. He brought them up to Boston and the Sons of Liberty read them aloud on the steps of Faneuil Hall.

With this revelation, the residents in Middleborough turned against the Loyalists. They verbally assaulted and eventually attacked members of the Oliver family. An angry mob of forty surrounded Oliver Hall, then torched and burned it to the ground. They next appeared at Peter's front door and gave him an ultimatum: he could take his family and escape with their lives or remain inside while they burned down his home. Peter, Sally, and their children fled to Boston and eventually reached London. They never returned to America and the Sons of Liberty took ownership of the house, then sold the family's furniture and belongings. They collected ammunition from Oliver's ironworks to supply the Minuteman Militia, where it may have been used in the famous battle on Lexington Green, memorialized as "the shot heard 'round the world.'"

The house is filled with antiques portraying life in the eighteenth century.

Peter Oliver's escape tunnel emerges inside the barn.

Oliver House passed down through six other families, most of whom had some form of tragedy occur within its walls. Judge Thomas Weston and his family kept it for thirty-six years. Weston left it to his daughter, Bethaniah, who married Earl Sproat. The Sproats lost two children in infancy, and six-year-old James died of pneumonia. Earle died of tuberculosis, but the worst tragedy befell young Abigail. At two years of age, she was scalded by a pot of boiling water and died in terrible pain from the resulting infection.

Henry Champion Jones bought the dwelling in 1893 and his family held it for fifty years. Peter Oliver, a descendant of the original family, purchased it in 1945 and restored it to its colonial-era decor. In 2016, it was purchased by the town of Middleborough.

Christy Parrish, an experienced investigator and local historian, is the caretaker for the Peter Oliver Estate. She gave us a quick tour of the grounds and offered some of the family history. She then shared some of her personal experiences dealing with its otherworldly occupants. She has heard disembodied voices several times including a very clear, "God save the King" in a British accent. One evening, after hosting an event, she locked up the building and walked outside to her car. She realized she had forgotten to turn off the electric candles, so she went back inside and climbed to the second floor. As she turned to leave, she saw a dark figure in her peripheral vision, then heard a male voice behind her say, "You came back." She decided not to continue the conversation.

Christy showed me a photo taken with her cell phone that displays a little dog once owned by the Sprouts appearing in a dressing mirror in Bethaniah's bedroom. In that same room, I took an infrared photo that reveals the impression of a face, floating near the rear entrance. Christy feels strongly that Bethaniah Sprout is the spirit most often encountered. She added, "She was born in the house and spent her entire life within its confines." Christy also encountered the full-bodied apparition of a Wampanoag warrior in the rear kitchen. He walked directly towards her, then turned and exited through a wall that formerly served as the servants' entrance.

The entire grounds are active, with many reports of flickering lights, luminous orbs floating above the hedges, and the percussive sound of Native drumbeats. Almost every paranormal group that has investigated Oliver House has a similar story, or some convincing audio evidence. The house has been featured on two paranormal TV shows. With its tragic and violent history, it is no surprise to find the estate suffused with trauma, continuing to live up to its supernatural reputation.

The estate of Dr. Peter Oliver and the manicured grounds that surround it were once populated by the indigenous Nemasket and Wampanoag tribes. Nemasket, in the Algonquian language, means "the place of fish." Their various Sachems held gatherings at nearby Muttock Hill, where they fished for herring and enjoyed a spectacular view of the harbor. Native trails utilized for trade ran throughout the northeast and seven of them intersected at the Nemasket River. Nearby, there are sacred burial sites that are estimated to hold the bodies of 1,500 Native Americans.

The Great Sachem Massasoit, who in 1620 befriended the Puritans at Plymouth Colony, held conferences on Muttock Hill with the other chieftains, and it was home to some of his extended family. When Massasoit contracted smallpox, his family brought him to Nemasket, where he spent his final days. It remained a favorite area for Metacomet, the son of Massasoit, to ride out the harsh New England winters. Better known by his Christian name, Philip, he later became the Sachem and incited the bloody

The playful laughter of children has been recorded in the second-floor bedrooms.

The formal sitting room, where Ben Franklin convinced Judge Oliver and Governor Hutchinson to confer with him on the night he acquired the incriminating letters.

uprising in 1675 known as King Philip's War. Eventually, the Nemasket tribe sold the land surrounding Muttock Hill to the colonists.

With her presentation completed, Christy encouraged us to explore the house on our own. It did not take long to experience something unusual. As we entered the dining room, we felt a sudden drop in temperature. The room registered 46 degrees for about thirty-five minutes, then returned to 68 degrees for the next few hours. For the remainder of the evening, no other room in the house registered less than 67 degrees.

The seven of us gathered in the sitting room at dusk and sat in silence for twenty minutes, listening for any unusual sounds. We heard a loud thump on the second story, followed by the sound of a ball rolling across the floor. A couple of us ran upstairs with a camera, only to find nothing out of place. We then proceeded from room to room, and with our recorders running, we asked questions about its former occupants. Nothing else happened for the next three hours, until we reached the children's bedroom on the second floor. At about 10:30 p.m., we clearly heard four footsteps ascending the servant's stairway leading to the central hallway. I turned my camera toward the doorway, expecting to see our visitor, but, of course, nobody emerged from the servant's entrance.

During our second investigation in September 2018, Michelle Ross spent time in the fieldstone basement, where she witnessed a blue orb float down the stairway and pass through the wall. On the second floor, Jeanie Foley, one of our sensitives felt a tightness in her chest in a room once occupied by young James Sproat, who had died from pneumonia. At about 10:00 p.m. we took a break and gathered on the first floor to compare notes. I walked back upstairs to check the batteries in my camera, then briefly chatted with Christy on the landing next to the hallway.

I had my back to the front of the house, but Christy had a good view of the entire landing. Her eyes suddenly widened, and she said that the silhouette of a woman had just walked behind me, from Sally's bedroom, across the landing, and into the Franklin Room. We ran into that room and found nothing, but as I turned back toward the hallway, I felt a surge of electrical current run up my right arm and linger at my shoulder. We concluded that the specter of Sally Hutchinson or Bethaniah Sprout may have passed right through my body.

We have investigated Oliver House four times, and this colonial-era treasure never disappoints. Its resident spirits are not the least bit hostile or unfriendly. I still consider it one of the most active locations that BPI has explored, and we cannot wait to get back there again.

Young Abigail Weston was fatally scalded by a pot of boiling water in the servant's kitchen.

The image of a face appears near the doorway of the bedroom once occupied by Sally Hutchinson.

3

MASS GRAVES AT DEER ISLAND

Paranormal investigators have different theories regarding haunted sites and their origins. One of the more commonly accepted is the "Stone Tape" theory, which suggests that extreme trauma can leave a permanent impression on the area in question. A wartime battle, a violent murder, or an unexpected death are examples that might leave an energy imprint that can still be detected hundreds of years later by mediums and sensitives.

Deer Island is one of those places. In the 1600s, it was a paradise of freshwater ponds, sleepy glades, and tidal flats enjoyed by the Native American tribes for centuries. Originally separated from the city of Winthrop by a strait at Point Shirley, conditions changed when the Great New England Hurricane of 1938 devastated the entire coastline. Its relentless gales filled in the narrow channel with sand, permanently connecting the island to the mainland.

Deer Island has seen more death than most major cities. It is estimated that some 1,600 bodies are interred within its 185 acres. As early as 1670, the Mass Bay Colonies designated the island as a quarantine station for immigrants and refugees arriving by ship, many of them suffering from typhus and smallpox. There are no existing fatality records for that era.

King Philip's War broke out in 1675, an inevitable clash between the colonies and the local tribes who gradually relinquished their claims to ancestral land. Despite a great number of Natives converting to Christianity, the English colonists still considered them dangerous. When hostilities erupted, the colonies gathered up between 500 and 1,000 "Praying Indians" from Natick, Concord, and Marlborough and relocated them to Deer Island. In the middle of the harsh, New England winter they had no shelter, inadequate clothing, and limited supplies. Those who did not succumb to the bitter cold fell victim to raiding parties that sold them off as slaves in the West Indies. No less than 600 unmarked Native graves are spread throughout the island.

Next came the "Coffin Ships" in the mid-1800s, as hordes of Irish immigrants fled the devastating effects of the Great Famine. In 1847 alone, during the peak of the famine years, no less than 25,000 Irish arrived in Boston. Some 5,000 of the sick and suffering were brought to improvised hospitals and triage areas on Deer Island. Most managed to survive and eventually make their way to Boston but almost 900 perished at the site.

The Deer Island Almshouse was built in 1853. (*Photograph by A. H. Folsom, 1926*)

A memorial has been added for the Native Americans imprisoned during King Philip's War in 1675.

On the northern portion of the island, Resthaven Cemetery contains the bodies of roughly 860 Irish immigrants in unmarked graves.

An almshouse caring for the poor and homeless population of Boston was established on Deer Island in 1853. Far ahead of its time, its facilities included a nursery, a school, a workshop, and a hospital. A second home was set up in 1858 for juvenile offenders, most of them boys, and a few years later they added the House of Reformation for Girls.

The Deer Island House of Industry stopped operating as a poorhouse when it began housing low-level offenders in the 1880s—those arrested for drunkenness or petty theft. It was converted to the House of Correction in 1896, when South Boston closed its prison and transferred their population to Deer Island. The prison operated for almost 100 years, finally closing its doors in 1991, when the building was demolished to allow construction of the Deer Island Wastewater Treatment plant, which currently occupies the site.

The House of Correction was involved in a controversial test of the influenza vaccine in 1918. Out of its 300 inmates, sixty-two volunteers were offered full pardons if they agreed to participate in the trial. Although none of the prisoners died as a result of the vaccine, the ward doctor succumbed to the deadly virus. There are no records of any prisoners having been pardoned.

At the outset of World War II, the US Army constructed Fort Dawes at Deer Island for the coastal defense of Boston Harbor. In 1941, they built the first access road on the northeast side of the island. During construction of the military base, many of the Irish immigrant's bodies were removed from the southern side and relocated to the New Resthaven Cemetery on the northern side. The Great Hunger Memorial, dedicated in May 2019, features a 16-foot Celtic cross honoring the 870 victims of the famine. On the northwest side, a plaque is dedicated to the members of the Nipmuc tribe imprisoned during King Philip's War.

In 2015, the body of a toddler was abandoned at Deer Island, later identified as three-year-old Bella Bond. Michael McCarthy, boyfriend of the child's mother, was charged and convicted of murder in the second degree. He was sentenced to life imprisonment.

Today, the island is encircled by a paved walkway offering views of Logan Airport and Boston Harbor. Beneath its 185 acres of grassy parkland lie the bodies of almost 2,000 immigrants, Native Americans, prisoners, indigents, and paupers.

Small wonder that it is haunted.

We conducted two investigations at Deer Island. In July 2021, we arrived with a small group and concentrated our energies on three areas, beginning near the entrance and finishing on the southern side, near the water treatment plant.

Just after dusk, we entered on the northern side, using the paved pathway that encircles the island. We had not gotten more than 30 yards in when Jacob Abbisso, our medium, sensed what he later described as some form of "Gatekeeper." It bore a resemblance to illustrations he had seen of the mythical golems created by Jewish mystics. This is a very unusual impression. He had never described anything like that before, or since. He felt it was not hostile or threatening, just quietly observing as we entered its domain (I am glad I could not see that).

Within that same area, he sensed the presence of a small group of Native Americans. They stood apart and watched from a distance but never attempted to communicate.

High above the northern side of Deer Island stands a memorial to the 800 victims of the Irish famine.

The almshouse was converted to the Suffolk County House of Correction in 1896. (*Photograph by A. H. Folsom, 1926*)

I really cannot blame them after the treatment they endured. We passed a tiny alcove, where Jacob reported feeling pressure in his head and then pain in his upper teeth. In that same area, Michelle Ross had a feeling that we were being watched. Both felt an increasing heaviness as we moved southward. We consulted the map of the island and realized we were nearing the New Resthaven Cemetery, where most of the Irish were interred. We only stayed there for a brief amount of time, as we wanted to stick to our game plan.

On the southern side of the island, Jacob received two, very strong impressions: one of a middle-aged woman with long brown hair wearing a dress with a flowery pattern, and an older man sporting a white, ragged beard. He leaned against a railing and stared out to sea. Jacob invited him to come closer, but he waved his hand in a very forlorn gesture, as if to say, "What's the point?" Jake felt this man had been a sailor or had some maritime connection.

We stopped there and tried a few EVP sessions. Michelle felt herself drawn to the top of the hill overlooking the pathway, so we climbed up there and decided to conduct a Spirit Box session. The SB-7 swept through its frequencies, every now and then spitting out a brief word or two in between the static, but nothing clear enough to consider a communication. We had turned off the Spirit Box and were just talking, when all three of us felt a sudden chill. At that exact instant, Jacob saw a static charge coming off my baseball hat. It was clear that we were not alone, but the spirits made no further efforts to be heard.

We moved along to the southwestern portion until we passed the water treatment plant. We had traversed about three-quarters of the outer pathway, so we settled down on the western side, near the Irish Memorial for one last EVP session. This area did not feel as active, but you never know—things can change rapidly. Upon later review, the final session produced nothing of interest, but we had identified at least two promising areas for our future investigations.

We concluded that Deer Island is a place of extraordinary beauty and supreme tragedy. Never have we experienced a setting like this, infused with the pain and suffering of so many different victims. I believe that every inch of this tiny island is suffused with some form of trauma.

The paved walking path, shot with infrared photography, encircles the entire island.

Prisoners at the South Boston House of Correction were transferred to Deer Island in 1896. (*Photograph taken in 1910*)

4

FORSAKEN RUTLAND PRISON CAMP

I have been to Rutland Prison Camp several times and there is something different about this abandoned site, something very dark. I am not alone in that assessment. Sure, no prison has ever been a peaceful place; most often they are full of anger, frustration, and violence, but this prison was not like all the others. It was a working farm and served more as a rehabilitation facility than a punitive one. The camp was established in 1903 in the rural town of Rutland, Massachusetts, on the former site of Captain Phineas Walker's farm. Walker cleared the land in 1750 and named it Elm Tree Farm, inspired by a giant elm that stood proudly at its entrance. That ancient tree is long gone, taken down by Dutch Elm disease in 1924. Northwest Rutland at the time was called New Boston. Captain Walker fought in the Revolutionary War and later served in the Rutland town offices. He passed away in 1792 at the age of seventy-one. His family held the land through the Civil War years and then sold the 900 acres to the Commonwealth.

When the Prison Camp opened in 1904 under the leadership of Superintendent William Witham, they made use of an existing barn, the Walker farmhouse, and the former New Boston schoolhouse. In April, sixteen prisoners convicted of minor offenses were transferred from various prisons and Witham greeted them with his unique vision. Rather than wasting away inside a dreary cell, his prisoners would sleep on clean mattresses inside a dormitory and were expected to work each day on some aspect of the farm. They had roll call at 5:00 p.m. and enjoyed yard privileges until 9:00. The farm encompassed 150 acres and included a dairy barn housing sixty Holsteins, chicken coops, fields for planting various crops, and a garden where turnips, carrots, onions, and potatoes were grown. The farm turned a healthy profit by selling milk and eggs to the City of Worcester and supplying potatoes to the state prison system.

The work could be hard; some prisoners cleared land, cut down trees, dug ditches for foundations, or trenches for sewage. As long as the inmates obeyed the rules, they were well fed and treated with respect. For those who defied them, a cement cell block holding six claustrophobic units was utilized for solitary confinement. Although they had ample opportunity, the men rarely tried to escape, but the few who did were usually apprehended and returned. The average prison sentence might be as short as two weeks or as long as one year. Quoted in a news article in 1934, Charles Martin, one of the guards, stated that prisoners often stopped by his house after work for a drink and a piece of pie. On weekends, prisoners sometimes played baseball against the local teenagers.

The cell block held six cramped isolation cells.

So, why such negative vibes? One theory may explain that. In 1907, a small hospital was built on the site to treat prisoners who suffered from tuberculosis. These men came from statewide, maximum-security prisons and some had been convicted of violent crimes. They did not mix with the general population and not all of them recovered. More than fifty prisoners were buried at nearby Rutland Prison Cemetery, with only a steel cross to mark their passing.

There are historical records indicating that the Continental Congress sent British and Hessian prisoners from the Revolutionary War to work at Captain Walker's farm long before it became a working prison. And, according to Prison Commissioner Frederick Pettigrove, a number of bodies were unearthed at the site while digging foundations for the new buildings. They were moved to Goose Hill Cemetery and, although never identified, one of them was likely the remains of a Native American of some stature, as he had been buried at the top of the hill. Bad karma.

After operating successfully for thirty years, drainage problems forced the state to close the facility in 1931. The farm was situated within the watershed for the newly created Quabbin Reservoir. The remaining prisoners were transferred to Norfolk Prison Colony and most of Rutland Prison Camp's buildings were demolished. All that remains of the prison are graffiti-covered solitary cell blocks, some stone slabs above their foundations, a couple of cement walls, a root cellar, and a vaulted service tunnel accessible by crawling through a hole in the foundation slab. These decaying conditions contribute to an overall feeling of despair.

I toured the camp in 2020 with my friend Steven Flaherty, who operates Seven Hills Ghost Hunting and Paranormal Research. Steve believes the camp is home to an aggressive

Aggressive EVPs have been captured in the root cellar.

Anonymous graves are marked with only a single cross.

spirit and has some evidence to support that. He has spent a lot of time down in the service tunnel, where he captured quite a few EVPs. As an experiment, he suspended a crucifix from the ceiling and left his digital recorder running overnight. When he reviewed the file, he was shocked to discover an angry voice spouting, "Somebody brought Jesus here."

I returned to the camp in August 2022 with a small team of investigators. We set up our gear in the root cellar, a dark cavern carved 60 feet into the hillside and supported by four granite columns. There is no electricity throughout the camp, yet my Mel-Meter registered 0.3 and 0.4 mG in the cellar. Kim Bowman and Michelle Ross had their recorders running for the entire session and, in response to one of Kim's questions, she received a vulgar proposition in a leering male voice. Michelle later reviewed her files and found two separate EVPs. The first was mostly garbled except for the word "help" and the second, captured an hour later, was laced with profanity. My two recorders, placed at opposite ends of the root cellar, ran for the full two hours with no results. I found it disturbing that these entities only targeted the women.

Next, we moved on to the cement structure that contained six solitary confinement cells. The cell block is now in crumbling disarray, its roof long gone, and some of the cell walls have been reduced to a pile of stone rubble. In the corner of one cell, we found the remains of two freshly killed pheasants. Hunters are allowed in this area during hunting season, and it is likely that one of their retrievers decided this would be a good spot to store his game. There is nothing paranormal about that, but, still, we found it a little unsettling. We slowly worked our way through all six of the cells and tried to initiate contact with its spectral residents. At one point, Michelle and I sat in different cells, separated by about 50 feet. I quietly listened while she asked the questions. About thirty minutes in, I heard Michelle shout, "What?" Then, she walked over to my cell and asked if I had called her name. I had not, of course, so we played back her recording and very clearly heard a male spirit shout, "Hey, Michelle!" Strangely enough, it sounded like my own voice!

These are the kind of baffling incidents that happen at Rutland Prison Camp. Every paranormal team that spends time there comes away with some unique form of evidence.

We worked our way over to the underground service tunnel beneath the former hospital. One side of the foundation has collapsed inward, and by climbing through a large cavity and then sliding down the cement slab, you can access the tunnel, which extends about 80 feet and then abruptly ends. Depending on the weather, the eastern portion is sometimes under a few inches of dripping water. There is also a gaping hole in the ceiling, a sure sign that the rest will come tumbling down, someday. Although other groups have reported paranormal activity in this area, none of our gadgets alerted us to changes in the environment, nor did we capture any EVPs.

We checked out the other ruins, then returned to the root cellar for one more try. Once again, Michelle's recorder caught a phantom voice, but it was faint and difficult to decipher. By that time, we were all ready to pack up and leave the prison camp. It is hard to define, but there is a certain heaviness felt by all of us inside that root cellar.

Some spirits are mischievous, some are angry and aggressive. This place seems to fall into both categories, but it seldom disappoints. We hope to get back there in the next year for another investigation. There are plans in motion to dismantle the camp completely, but for now it remains one of the more active locations in the area.

The root cellar has become a showplace for local graffiti artists.

Above left: Collapsed walls obscure the entrance to the underground tunnel.

Above right: A gaping hole in the ceiling of the tunnel causes it to flood during the spring.

5

SPECTERS AT THE PALACE THEATRE

Manchester, NH, is known as "The Queen City," and the Palace Theatre may well be its Crown Jewel.

In 1914, a young Victor Charas envisioned his grand theatre as a "palace of the arts and culture." Charas was a Greek immigrant who arrived in America at the age of twenty-four and worked his way to prominence in real estate. Inspired by the great New York City theatres, he hired well-respected architect Leon Lempert to design the interior.

The Palace Theatre opened to a packed house on April 9, 1915, featuring the musical comedy *Modern Eve*. Far ahead of its time, it was literally fireproof due to a 10-foot firewall between its neighboring buildings. Charas simulated air conditioning by placing giant blocks of ice in tunnels beneath the stage and using fans to circulate the air.

The venue thrived for the next fifteen years, hosting famous vaudeville performers such as Jimmy Durante, Bob Hope, the Marx Brothers, Red Skelton, and Harry Houdini. Stock theatre groups performed there daily, in front of packed audiences. During the Roaring Twenties, no less than twenty-two theatres graced downtown Manchester, but only the Palace managed to survive beyond the Great Depression.

The Palace Theatre's name was chosen from a contest won by a local resident, Amelia Sansoucie. Perhaps it should have been named The Phoenix. Like the bird of legend, it has risen from the ashes repeatedly, having miraculously survived 100 years of economic downturns, urban decay, a nine-alarm fire, two floods, a national depression, and a worldwide pandemic.

Silent pictures arrived in the 1920s, followed by the "talkies," all but sounding the death knell for vaudeville. The growing popularity of television contributed to the nationwide downfall of the great theatres. When the stock market crashed in 1929, leading to the Great Depression, businesses in downtown Manchester began shutting down, and the area once known as a center for the arts turned more and more desolate.

Victor Charas died in 1935, and his son, George, converted the Palace to a movie house. At its lowest point, the theatre survived by showing X-rated movies. Later, it was used for classes at New Hampshire College, but the school moved to a new campus, and the Palace fell into years of disrepair. When George died in 1965, the building was sold to a local butcher, its seats removed, and the historic theatre converted to warehouse space. It came very close to being demolished for construction of a parking garage.

The Palace Theatre has operated continuously since 1915.

In the 1970s, Manchester enjoyed a cultural resurgence. Local attorney John McLane and Mayor Sylvio Dupuis spearheaded the creation of The Palace Theatre Trust, which raised enough cash to renovate and restore the iconic building to its original grandeur, an 834-seat performing arts center. On November 7, 1974, the Palace finally reopened with a performance of *Madame Butterfly*.

In 1980, a rusted water pipe burst, sending 70,000 gallons of water surging over the balcony, and flooding the entire theatre. A nine-alarm fire in 1984 threatened to destroy the entirety of Hanover Street, but the Palace's sturdy firewall stopped the spread of flames and allowed Manchester firefighters to get control of the blaze. The League of Historic American Theatres in 2012 awarded the Palace with the Outstanding Historic Theatre Award. Like many other venues, the Palace shut its doors at the outset of the 2020 pandemic but managed to reopen in June 2021.

But, what of its ghosts? Although the building survived some extreme challenges, there are no records of any deaths within its confines. There seem to be three different entities at play. Employees and patrons have most often described a young girl in a white dress who floats above the balcony. There is nothing threatening about her, and she sometimes smiles at them. During the filming of a *Ghost Hunters* TV

The interior features ornate, turn-of-the-century decor.

show at the Palace, it was revealed that, in 1984, a woman in the next building had perished in a fire.

Patrons often feel they are being watched, particularly in the ladies' room. The current owner, Peter Ramsey, has had a few encounters with its resident spirit. One night, before closing, he had secured the bathroom doors open to prevent the pipes from freezing. As he turned to leave, both doors simultaneously slammed shut.

Artistic director Carl Rajotte described how the toilets in the ladies' room, which utilize motion detectors, constantly flush, although nobody is in the room. They had the *Ghost Hunters* film crew monitoring it, when they heard one of the stalls flushing. The camera man swung open the stall door and they witnessed a glowing sphere of light rise above the stall and fly into the hallway. Carl has worked there for twenty years, and he took a photograph in the boiler room that appears to show a young girl wearing a white dress with a red sash. They believe she is the spirit of Emma Bechert, one of their child actors who passed away in 2007 at the age of fourteen. The theatre dedicated a special seat to Emma in the third row, marked by a gold plaque with her name inscribed. Carl showed me a second photograph he had taken that displayed the face of a young child seated in that very spot. Theatre employees have heard footsteps on the staircase, and the locked doors leading to the balcony rattling so loudly that Carl felt compelled to shout, "Sorry! We're closed!" Once, at 1:00 a.m., he described the sounds of a phantom orchestra warming up for a performance.

On another occasion, he had worked late into the night and was about to lock up the building. Carl had turned off and unplugged his CD player. Seconds after he left the room,

Two apparitions have been seen standing atop the balcony.

the player came back to life, blaring out loud music from the middle of a track. He quickly left the building. When he returned the following morning, it was still unplugged.

Jeff Carcia and I investigated the Palace in September 2023. We placed six infrared cameras in strategic locations, then conducted EVP sessions on the balcony, on the stage, in the lower audience, the boiler room, two hallways, and the dressing rooms. In the boiler room, the motion detector sounded an alert, although neither of us were moving. We managed to record the sound of the balcony doors being rattled, and clear footsteps descending into the cellar, but two theatre employees were inside the building, so we consider it inconclusive evidence.

I have been to quite a few haunted theatres, and it is my belief that spirits are attracted by the positive vibrations created by artistic and creative performers, and this powerful energy may have infused the venue. Local actor George Piehl once said, "The Palace Theatre has a soul. Part of it comes from the architecture, like being in a cathedral. And, as you sit there, looking at the stage, you can't help but feel the history."

There is something special about the Palace Theatre. As Bob Shea, executive director in the early '90s, said: "There's something sacred and holy about these cultural institutions, a theatre like the Palace, or a gallery like the Currier. Art is magic. It's a secular religion in a way. They've hosted so many events and great, creative work, you just feel it emanate from the building itself."

Can a building have a soul? Perhaps the theater itself is the venerable presence experienced by so many of its patrons.

The Palace is a beautifully restored 834-seat performance center.

Constructed with sturdy oak and gilded with gold leaf, the theatre closely resembles its New York namesake.

Above left: A photograph taken in the boiler room reveals what appears to be a young girl wearing a white dress. (*Photo by Artistic Director, Carl Rajotte*)

Above right: A flash of light appears in the seat dedicated to a deceased child actor. A second apparition leans over the box seats. (*Photo by Carl Rajotte*)

Right: The boiler room often displays paranormal activity.

6

DEATH AT THE VICTORIAN MANSION

Your first look at the S.K. Pierce Mansion will convince you that it is haunted. It is the type of building directors choose for the setting of Gothic horror movies, a Victorian-style, three-story behemoth with a belfry looming above a mansard roof. Its nineteenth-century grandeur features twenty-six rooms, 11-foot ceilings, two marble fireplaces, a grand staircase, and elaborate, hand-carved woodwork throughout. I half expected Lurch to answer the front door.

Located in Gardner, Massachusetts, it is consistently listed among the most haunted locations in America and there is plenty of supporting evidence. In its heyday, it was host to some famous personalities including Bette Davis, Norman Rockwell, Calvin Coolidge, and Fats Domino. The current owners have rebranded it as the Haunted SK Pierce Victorian Mansion with plans to convert it to a horror-themed attraction for Halloween, but for now they offer it for overnight investigations by paranormal groups.

We investigated the mansion in April 2022. Our host and caretaker, Marion Luoma, took us on a quick tour of the interior while relaying some of the building's macabre history. She knew the previous owners quite well. Her family has been involved with the estate for many years and experienced the full gamut of paranormal phenomena, including footsteps, phantom voices, slamming doors, knocking sounds, and shadow figures. As the house was unoccupied while renovations went on, it became a playground for some of their children. Marion's nephew has vowed never to set foot in the mansion again. When he was a child, he had been hiding in one of the closets when he felt a pair of hands grab him forcefully by the shoulders and shove him out into the hallway.

Marion was present when a camera crew for one of the paranormal TV shows conducted their initial walk-through. One of the videographers was standing on the landing above the back stairway and making jokes about the spirits. Marion saw him lifted off his feet, hurled over the banister, and dropped 10 feet to the stairs below. Note to self: do not provoke the ghosts.

Sylvester Knowlton Pierce amassed his fortune by manufacturing chairs. At the age of twenty-five, he purchased an existing chair factory that operated across the street from the future site of the mansion. The business became so profitable that Gardner, for a time, was known as "Chair City."

In 1875, Pierce hired prominent Worcester architect E. Boynton to design and build the 7,000-square-foot masterpiece. The project was completed in two years and Sylvester

The upright piano is a unique example of Victorian-era instruments.

Eighteenth-century furniture graces the second-floor landing.

7

SPIRITS ABOARD THE USS SALEM

The Ionian Islands, also known the Heptanes, are situated on the west coast of Greece. In 1953, nearly 115 earthquakes wreaked havoc in the region between the islands Kefalonia and Zakynthos. The largest and most devastating quake struck on August 12, measuring 7.2 on the surface wave magnitude scale, and it raised the entire surface of Kefalonia almost 24 inches. Ithaca, Kefalonia, and Zakynthos took the worst of it, with loss of life estimated at 800 and countless additional victims left homeless, hungry, and frightened.

The quake is often described as the worst tragedy in Greek history. Gas lines were exposed, raging fires broke out, and frequent explosions rocked the eastern side of Zakynthos. Victims fled the collapsing structures, many were burned or crushed to death, others were trapped beneath the rubble. Building damage was extensive, and the southern islands of Zakynthos and Kefalonia were practically leveled. Only two buildings remained standing in the capital city of Zakynthos.

As desperate calls went out for help, British Royal Navy vessels and Israeli warships were the first to arrive, providing emergency medical aid, food, and water. The USS *Salem* pulled into port and immediately set up a triage and a makeshift hospital, rushing aboard victims suffering from broken limbs, head injuries, and horrible burns. The medical crew stabilized the wounded, performed emergency surgery, and gave comfort to the dying. The death toll kept mounting and the *Salem* stored hundreds of bodies in its morgue. The ship remained through October 9, when their supplies ran out and they were relieved by the *Des Moines*.

Soon after they departed the Ionian Islands, the *Salem* began reporting disturbing incidents in all areas of the ship. Sailors heard tortured voices calling for help, witnessed dark, shadowy figures walking the decks, heard frightened screams emanate from the hospital area, and the mess hall situated above the morgue was sometimes filled with an acrid, burning scent.

The *Salem* is a *Des Moines*-class heavy cruiser, one of three built at the end of World War II. It was constructed by Bethlehem Steel in the Fore River shipyard in Quincy, Massachusetts, and launched in March 1947. Vice Admiral John C. Daniel, who served in both World War II and the Korean War, became her first captain. The USS *Salem* served a ten-year career as flagship of the U.S. Sixth Fleet in the Mediterranean and the Second Fleet in the Atlantic. Although heavily armed with 8-inch semiautomatic guns, she never saw battle but was deployed around the world for military exercises.

The USS *Salem* is one of three existing *Des Moines*-class heavy cruisers.

Although heavily armed, the *Salem* never saw combat.

The ship was decommissioned in January 1959. She found her way to Quincy Harbor in 1994 and was converted to the Unites States Naval Shipbuilding Museum. Visitors can tour it for a reasonable fee. It is the only heavy cruiser still operating and the last of its class to be decommissioned. The *Salem* was nicknamed "the Sea Witch" after docking briefly in the Witch City.

In June 2022, Boston Paranormal conducted an investigation on-board the USS *Salem*. Our host, Don DeCristofaro, a veteran of the U.S. Navy, is also an experienced investigator with over twenty years in the field. He is a founding member of the Greater Boston Paranormal Associates and has been leading paranormal groups aboard the ship since 2000.

He stated: "When we give tours, we can't guarantee that something is going to happen, but it's a very rare night when nothing happens on the *Salem*." Don has spent thousands of hours aboard the ship and experienced the full gamut of phenomena. He is completely convinced that its ghosts are real and has the physical evidence to back it up. His team has recorded numerous EVPs over the years, they have heard disembodied voices, and some of them call him by name.

Interviewed countless times about the *Salem*, Don had an interesting observation. He said that in 2009, the Atlantic Paranormal Society (TAPS) arranged an investigation for their television show, and ever since that night, the activity on-board has increased tenfold. "It's almost as if they had opened several doors for spirits on the ship," he said. "And they never closed them when they left."

"My most intense experiences have been in the ward room and the mess decks. We spent an evening in the ward room where several chairs were overturned," he recalls. "That night was the only time I can honestly say I was uncomfortable on the ship. I really felt like something bad was with us that night."

Quite a variety of spirits remain on-board the *Salem*. There is a seven-year-old girl named Lucy, who died with her family in Greece. Another entity named Nikko searches endlessly for his wife and family, lost in the earthquake. A mischievous spirit they call "The Peeker" often peers around corners and doorways.

Retired Marine John Connor is the ship's head archivist and has an office aboard the *Salem*. He often hears disembodied voices and once heard his name called out as he passed through the sailors' sleeping quarters. "Sometimes I'll hear footsteps in those rooms, and I look but there's nobody there," he said. "It doesn't bother me, but you often get the feeling that there is someone watching you. You get chills running up your spine."

In recent years, Don has done extensive research into the sailors who served aboard the ship. Using naval records and crew listings for each deployment of the *Salem*, Don and his team have managed to identify quite a few of the spirits. He is now convinced that only some of them died in the Ionian earthquake. The *Salem* has suffered tragic accidents of its own over the years.

In 1954, the *Salem* had been moored in Boston when an explosion occurred aboard the USS *Leyte*, killing 300 sailors. Many injured in the blast were rushed to the *Salem*'s hospital for treatment, but several of them died. It happened again in 1956, when a gun mount exploded on the destroyer USS *John R. Pierce*. Some of the wounded sailors were brought aboard the *Salem*, where they succumbed to injuries.

Frank O'Brien, machinist first class, is often seen in the hospital area, as is Ralph Mellott, gunner's mate, who died in the USS *John R. Pierce* explosion. The ghost who peeks around corners is now believed to be Curtis Cochrane, who died in a fall in the

Right: Surgeons saved many of the earthquake victims, but others died on the operating table.

Below: In a ship this large and complex, there are unforeseen accidents and injuries.

hangar passageway. Gunner's Mate William Austin is believed to have suffered a head injury on the number three turret. He usually communicates in the mess hall.

The entity known as "The Chief" has a long-term relationship with Don. They believed he had been the ship's cook since they often encounter him in the third mess hall. He is fiercely dedicated to the *Salem* and has been known to complain that he is the only one working. Using mediums, psychics, and electronic tools, they have recently identified "The Chief" as RML George Parker. During a filming for the *Kindred Spirits* show, Don asked "The Chief" to weigh in and was rewarded by a very clear EVP laced with profanity. Don theorizes that George died in another location but returned to watch over the *Salem*, because that is where he felt at home.

Two of the sailors who remain on-board served on different ships but came from the same hometown. Their lifelong connection appears to have brought them together in death. The GBPA team has located, and posted photographs of the crewmen, and been rewarded for their efforts by increased communication; it seems the ghosts are pleased to be remembered.

The mess hall is located right above the morgue, where 400 bodies had been stored during the earthquake evacuation. Don suggested that we concentrate on that area. He also mentioned a phantom dog that roams the storied vessel. "He likes to climb onto the bunks and snuggle up to the person sitting there," he said. "I've felt him brush up against me a few times."

Since we had such a large area to explore, we split up into smaller groups to cover more ground. Below the main deck, the *Salem* turns into a veritable maze of steel corridors, open hatchways, access ladders, and interconnected chambers. There are mess halls, sleeping quarters, a dentist's office, an operating theater, museum displays, officers' quarters, and an engine room.

Footsteps and phantom voices haunt the sleeping quarters for the crew.

As we explored the ship, both groups heard unusual noises: a scratching sound emanating from the lockers, a low moan outside of the operating theater, and loud knocks coming from empty rooms off the corridors.

While sitting quietly in the corridor outside the officers' mess, Cynthia and Michelle Ross both heard a faint whisper in a male voice, but they could not make out the words. Michelle later recorded footsteps in the same hallway.

At the front of the ship, near the windlass, Jacob Abbisso and Shane Ross had set a REM Pod on the floor between two K-II meters. Our camera feed caught all three of them lighting up in succession, as if somebody had walked down the corridor. One of her audio files produced the sound of a wave crashing. The sea was extremely calm that night, and the *Salem* was moored in a tranquil harbor, so that was unlikely, if not impossible. Just to make sure, Michelle ran up on-deck to see if the conditions had changed; she found only calm seas.

We also caught the sound of a barking dog, but the ship was close enough to the dock for it to have been a living dog. There are no residential homes nearby, but we could not rule out a natural explanation. Then again, who walks their dog late at night, in a dark and desolate harbor? At the end of the night, we gathered in the aft mess hall for one final EVP session. We captured no phantom voices, but out in the corridor, the REM Pod sounded three times.

In a single evening, we had come away with enough physical evidence to convince me that the *Salem*'s reputation is well deserved. It is one of the most haunted vessels in the country.

 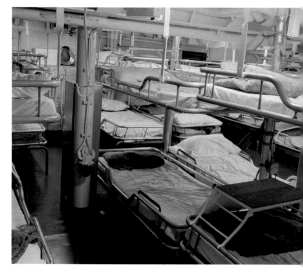

Above left: An aggressive spirit was encountered in the officers' mess hall.

Above right: The ship's hospital is one of the most active areas.

8

BANCROFT CASTLE AND GIBBET HILL

Groton, a quaint New England town established in 1655, is one of the most idyllic areas in Massachusetts. Take a leisurely drive through it, and you will pass old colonial homes, charming white churches, working farms, and a rolling hillside that overlooks the town center.

Just above the crest of Gibbet Hill are the remains of an abandoned castle featuring fieldstone walls, a 60-foot observation tower, and a crumbling, ivy-covered courtyard. In daylight, it presents a bucolic scene with spectacular views of Groton, Mount Wachusett, and the surrounding countryside. Children play inside the castle and newly married couples pose for wedding pictures.

At night, it takes on a different feel. There are numerous ghost stories attached to the hill and castle. For years, Groton residents have reported seeing colonial spirits, uniformed soldiers, Native Americans, and one man claimed that he looked through a tower window and saw a severed foot.

Groton has a long and tragic history. It was the site of violent skirmishes between early colonists and the Nipmuc tribe during King Philip's War. In March 1676, most of the town was burned to the ground while the settlers fled to nearby Concord. In 1694, the Abenaki tribe ransacked Groton, murdering an entire family. A few years later, three children from the Tarbell family were captured by Abenaki warriors during Queen Anne's War, then traded to a Mohawk village in 1707. They were assimilated into a tribe near Montreal and never returned to Groton.

There has even been a case of demonic possession in Groton, a servant girl named Elizabeth Knapp, who was examined and treated by the Reverend Samuel Willard in 1670. She later went on to live a traditional Puritan life, married and bore ten children.

In the early 1900s, the town was a focal point for Ku Klux Klan activities promoting anti-Catholic sentiment and hatred for ethnic minorities. In September 1924, the Klansmen held a gathering of approximately fifty cars containing hooded professionals and local merchants. The townsfolk opposed the Klan and their active protest resulted in a violent confrontation. Two years later, a group of 400 Klansmen were meeting in a Groton field and were fired upon by a large group of townspeople enraged by their racist views. The police reported no casualties.

The stone sections of the castle are all that remain since 1932, when the Groton Hunt Club burned to the ground.

The castle was designed by Italian masons.

Near the top of Gibbet Hill, an ancient oak tree stands, silhouetted against the open sky. Groton residents believe it was used for hangings in the 1600s. The term "Gibbet" refers to a gallows-like structure designed for public executions. It is more likely that the town named it after Gibbet Hill in England. However, there is mention of one such incident in early, colonial records. Town Clerk Richard Sawtell, while filing a land grant in 1665, stated that the hill was named Gibbet because they had captured, and publicly hung one of the Native combatants at the summit.

The mysterious castle was designed by Italian masons and built as a retirement home for wealthy businessman and Groton native William Bancroft. A brigadier general during the Spanish-American War, Bancroft became the first president of the Boston Elevated Railroad and served as the mayor of Cambridge in the 1890s. He began construction of his hilltop home in 1906, planning to call it "Shawfieldmont." He managed to complete only the tower and its attached bungalow, before running out of funds. For the next twelve years, he lived in the bungalow while adding to the castle, but in 1918, he decided to sell the property to local physician, Harold Ayers.

Ayers converted the structure into a sanatorium, where patients suffering from tuberculosis could enjoy the fresh air and restful countryside, while receiving treatment at Ayers' medical facility, the Groton Private Hospital. However, the 1930s brought about the Great Depression and the hospital was forced to close.

The Groton Hunt Club used the building for social activities, lavish banquets, formal soirees, and fox-hunting parties until 1932, when a Fourth of July fireworks display went out of control, setting fire to the clubhouse. The wooden structures burned to the ground, but the stone ruins of the castle remained standing.

In 1947, Marion Campbell, whose father owned the *Atlantic Monthly*, purchased the rundown farm with plans to breed Black Angus cattle. By 1980, the Campbells had bred more than 600 cattle. In 2000, a local builder attempted to purchase the site for creation of a seventy-eight home, residential development. However, Groton resident Steven Webber, the founder and CEO of Geotel Communications, believed that Gibbet Hill should belong to the town. He purchased the 500 acres of cattle farm and adjacent apple orchard and turned it into conservation land.

The Webber family retained 6 acres of farmland and they continue to raise cattle. At the base of the hillside, they operate a popular restaurant, The Gibbet Hill Grill. In recent years, they converted the 100-year-old barn next door to a multilevel function hall.

On a cold October night in 2020, we set out to investigate Bancroft Castle. We hiked up the steep trail at dusk and approached the castle, just as the last rays of sunlight were striking the turrets of the tower. Once the sun went down, the observation tower and fieldstone courtyard created long deep shadows that obscured our vision and contributed to the castle's eerie atmosphere.

We split into two groups. Michelle Ross and Topher Cooper began at the base of the observation tower, while Gina Bova and I explored the castle's interior and courtyard. We moved about the site and conducted four different EVP sessions, mentioning the names of previous owners, hoping to get their attention. In the eastern corner of the castle floor, the EMF suddenly spiked to 6.0 mG. We focused our attention on that area for another hour, but it supplied no further evidence.

As she climbed the hillside leading to the tower, Michelle experienced a strong feeling of vertigo. It soon dispelled, and she and Topher settled in at the base of the tower and

General Bancroft completed the tower and bungalow before running out of funds.

The remains of a fireplace are still visible on the second story.

conducted three EVP sessions. Even in the moonlight, the hexagon-shaped tower is impressive. Seven-foot windows look out on each of its three levels, and a circular turret adds to the feudal appearance. The roof is open to the stars, and you can see remnants of a fireplace that once existed on the second floor.

Topher and Michelle invoked a series of names we had discovered in our research. They asked about the castle and its various incarnations, but there did not appear to be any paranormal activity. EMF remained at zero until just after 10:00 p.m., when Michelle's REM Pod went off twice within a minute. They continued with their questions at the base of the tower for another hour. At that point, they decided to play back some of their recorded audio, but they found no ghostly voices.

Next, we explored the grounds behind the tower and noted consistently strong EMF readings in just one spot on the hillside. Less than a mile away, we could see a cell tower rising above the horizon. Since these towers are known to emit microwaves at a very high frequency, we speculated that our Mel-Meter was reacting to radio waves. Sure enough, we could literally draw a straight line between the tower, the hillside, and the corner of the castle where we had also recorded high EMF.

We had spent roughly five hours examining the site and came away with very little evidence of a haunting. That does not rule out the existence of ghosts at Gibbet Hill. An area that has experienced so much trauma is more than likely to harbor spirits, and a follow-up investigation could yield completely different results.

For now, we were grateful to have experienced the feudal charm and Gothic beauty of this unique location. I consider Bancroft Castle to be a New England treasure.

The stone turrets contribute to the castle's medieval appearance.

The picturesque courtyard has become a popular background for wedding photographers.

In the 1920s, the castle served as a sanitarium.

9

FORT WARREN AND THE LADY IN BLACK

The Lady in Black is one of the most famous ghosts in New England lore, a striking figure who is often seen standing high atop the arch at the entrance to Fort Warren, her black garment flowing in the wind, as she gazes wistfully across Boston Harbor, trapped there for all of eternity.

Although the legend was born before the twentieth century, it was historian and author Edward Snow who embellished the tale in his book *The Romance of Boston Bay*, published in 1944. He wrote the story hoping to save the 150-year-old fort from destruction and, in order to publicize the book, he conducted his own tours on Georges Island, accompanied by actors in Civil War uniforms.

In Snow's version, Confederate soldier Samuel Lanier was imprisoned at Fort Warren in 1861. He was able to smuggle a letter out to his wife, Melanie, who traveled from Georgia and concocted a bold plan to procure his release. She cut her hair, dressed herself as a man, and carried with her a pistol, a rope, and a pickax. With the assistance of local sympathizers, she borrowed a small rowboat and, in the dead of night, rowed from the mainland of Hull to Georges Island. She then crept ashore, hid in the bushes near the wall of the fort, and waited for a prearranged signal. When she heard a familiar, southern song whistled softly from within the fort, she tossed the rope over the wall and climbed inside. With the help of the other rebel prisoners, they started digging an escape tunnel, but they got too close to the Union soldiers' barracks. The scraping sounds alerted the sleeping soldiers, who quickly arrived at the scene. Melanie aimed her pistol at an officer, but he grabbed her wrist and the shot instead struck and killed her husband. She was captured and sentenced to hang on the following morning. Devastated by the tragic accident, she made only one request, that she be hanged wearing women's clothing. The soldiers complied but could only find a black robe, which she wore to her execution.

There are no military records or newspaper accounts in the 1860s that describe hangings at Fort Warren, but the legend persists. In August 1863, six prisoners did manage to escape, although two were caught before they left the island. Of the other four, two were apprehended while attempting to sail to Canada and the last two drowned offshore.

Tales of spectral figures roaming the island have been told since the fort was first constructed. At night, it can be a foreboding site, with stormy seas crashing on the rocks

The ferry disembarks at the main entrance to the 150-year-old fort.

below, and the New England wind whipping through the fort's hallways and courtyards. Numerous paranormal incidents have occurred over its 150 years. Ghostly soldiers in blue and gray uniforms have been witnessed by park rangers and tour guides. Others have heard a woman sobbing and seen footsteps in the snow that end abruptly in the middle of a clearing. Visitors have seen orbs of light floating across the courtyard, heard moaning voices, phantom footsteps, seen shadowy figures, and even heard a harmonica playing "John Brown's Body," a popular song in the South.

Fort Warren was constructed between 1833 and 1861, completed at the start of the Civil War. It is shaped like a pentagon, and its footprint covers most of the 28-acre Georges Island. The fort is named for Dr. Joseph Warren, a Revolutionary War hero who sent Paul Revere on his famous ride to warn the Minutemen. Warren later died at the Battle of Bunker Hill. During the Civil War, the fort served as a training ground for Union soldiers. The interior jail housed Northern political prisoners and Confederate soldiers, including their vice president, Alexander Stephens. The fort defended Boston Harbor through two world wars, finally being decommissioned in 1947. Because its first commander, Colonel Justin Dimick, believed in humane treatment for prisoners, their mortality rate was the lowest among any of the prison camps during the Civil War. Still, thirteen of the 1,000 prisoners housed at Fort Warren are buried on the grounds. Samuel Lanier is listed as one of them. Perhaps he still walks the island by night in search of his beloved Melanie.

In September 2022, we explored the fort. As it is such an expansive venue, we decided to concentrate on the areas where activity had been noted. Our cameras and recorders produced no physical evidence, but as we walked through a series of interconnected chambers on the second story, Michelle Ross saw the shadow of a figure in the doorway to a corner room. We walked into the chamber to find it completely empty. Near that

Jail cells where Confederate prisoners were held.

Phantom voices have been heard on the lower levels of the soldiers' barracks.

same area, Jacob Abbisso sensed the presence of three spirits. One presented the image of a middle-aged officer in uniform, wearing oval-shaped glasses, with a gold eagle pinned to his chest. He described the soldier as confident and slightly cocky, as if he had seen combat and wanted you to know it. The other spirits quickly faded before Jacob could discern any details. Later in the day, we joined up with Topher Cooper and explored the barracks, guard house, powder house, and jail cells. Sadly, there was no sighting of the Lady in Black, but enough spiritual contact to convince me that Georges Island is indeed haunted.

Fort Warren was named a National Historic Site in 1958 and is now part of the Boston Harbor Islands National Park. Visitors can take a ferry from Long Wharf and spend the day exploring the fort, while enjoying a spectacular view of Boston Light, the oldest lighthouse in the country. The extensive site offers a grassy courtyard, soldiers' barracks, prison cells, mess rooms, ammunition magazines, battlements, officer's quarters, and cannon turrets. For those feeling more adventurous, you can descend to the Corridor of Dungeons beneath the interior bastions and explore dimly lit tunnels that are cast in stark shadows.

The last ferry departs the island at dusk. You may not want to be stranded at Fort Warren when night falls.

Fort Warren was completed at the start of the Civil War.

Above left: We encountered two spirits in the second-story officers' quarters.

Above right: Visitors can spend hours exploring the courtyard, barracks, guard houses, and a literal maze of interior chambers.

The lowest level is known as the Corridor of Dungeons.

10

HEARTBREAK AT THE WAYSIDE INN

This haunting tale is a love story. The determined spirit of a young woman who frequents the Wayside Inn, a stunning, colonial tavern built in the early 1700s, has been linked to the story of her broken heart since her tragic death in 1842. Guests and employees alike have witnessed the spectral image of the innkeeper's daughter, Jerusha Howe, tall, elegant, wearing a blue dress, and shrouded by an air of sadness. She died at forty-four, still waiting for the Englishman who stole her heart and promised to return.

Established in 1716, Longfellow's Wayside Inn served as a stagecoach stop on the Boston Post Road, a direct route from New York City to Boston. One of America's earliest taverns, it proudly stands in the idyllic countryside of Sudbury, Massachusetts, having maintained much of its colonial charms—traditional decor, period furnishings, and many historic structures for visitors to enjoy, including a working grist mill, icehouse, a chapel, and the Redstone Schoolhouse, commonly believed to have served as the inspiration for the poem "Mary Had a Little Lamb."

In 1661, English settler John Howe owned a tavern in Marlborough, which he passed down to his son, Samuel. During King Philip's War, a year-long Native American rebellion in 1675, Samuel's home was set afire and destroyed. He then purchased the lot in Sudbury where the Wayside Inn now stands. Samuel deeded the property to his son, David, who built a two-room home where he and his wife, Hephzibah, welcomed travelers. Three more generations of Howes would keep the innkeeper's legacy alive.

Originally called Howe's Tavern, the inn was later made famous by the poet Henry Wordsworth Longfellow, who had been suffering a bout of writer's block after his wife perished in a fire in 1861. His publisher suggested that he get away and spend some time in the countryside. Inspired by its rustic charms and the interesting people he met at the tavern, he penned "*Tales of a Wayside Inn.*" Included in the iconic collection was "Paul Revere's Ride," although Longfellow had considered "The Landlord's Tale" as a working title.

When David's son, Ezekiel Howe, inherited the inn, he added the west kitchen and back parlor, doubling the size of the venue, and in 1744, he renamed it the Red Horse Tavern. Ezekiel was a lieutenant colonel in the Revolutionary War, and he often made use of the tavern to meet with his commanders. Ezekiel handed it down to Adam Howe, and in 1830 Adam left it to Lyman Howe, the last of the family innkeepers.

The Wayside Inn has welcomed travelers since 1716.

On the second floor, colonial-era displays portray life in eighteenth-century America.

Lyman was called the "Squire of Sudbury" and was known to abuse alcohol. His sister, Jerusha, was a refined, educated woman who supported the arts. She welcomed visitors and entertained guests, essentially running the inn for Lyman. Rooms nine and ten were originally her sleeping and sitting rooms. Jerusha never married but was socially involved throughout the area. She owned the first piano in Sudbury and often played it for guests at the inn. Her favorite piece was "The Copenhagen Waltz." In her time, she was affectionately known as the "Belle of Sudbury." Lyman had no heirs, and when he died in 1861, the inn was converted to a boarding house.

In 1897, Edward Lemon, a wool merchant, bought the entire lot, reopened the inn, and took advantage of Longfellow's fame to rename it Longfellow's Wayside Inn. After Edward died, his wife sold the inn to industrialist, Henry Ford of the Ford Auto Company. Ford was a historical preservationist, and the Ford Trust renovated the building to preserve its colonial charm. They also relocated the red schoolhouse and three other historic structures from around the country to the Sudbury compound.

If you are lucky enough to sleep in room nine, you may get more than you bargained for. Visitors are often awakened in the night by phantom footsteps, the haunting sound of a piano playing, or the bathroom faucet turning itself on. Rooms nine and ten were part of David Howe's original two-story home.

There are no existing portraits of Jerusha, but she was considered lovely and had numerous suitors, with many offers of marriage. Local historians pieced together a theory, based on her diary entries. She met a young Englishman at a Sudbury ball; they fell in love and were engaged to be married. However, her fiancé sailed back to England on some unfinished business with the promise he would soon return. She pined away for years but never saw him again, finally passing away at the age of forty-four from tuberculosis.

Room nine, which Jerusha Howe once occupied, exhibits the highest level of paranormal activity.

The Wayside has established a unique custom known as "The Secret Drawer Society." It began with innkeeper Francis Koppeis in the 1950s, who used to leave candy and handwritten notes in the rooms for the children. Soon, other guests took up the tradition, leaving reviews for future visitors, hiding them in drawers, beneath the bed, and inside the crevices of the oak ceiling beams. In its 300 years, the current owner estimates that 5,000 notes had been written and left inside the rooms. Laura Anno, our current lead investigator at BPI, has studied the Wayside extensively. A few years ago, she began reading through the notes, looking for any mention of paranormal phenomena. She estimated that 400 of the notes describe some kind of encounter or disturbance in Jerusha's rooms.

Paranormal teams have obtained plenty of evidence in room nine. In 2012, BPI used an infrared camera to capture a human-shaped shadow, drifting across the wall at 3:30 a.m. Another crew recorded faint piano music and later identified it as "The Battle of Prague," which, according to our research, was another favorite of Jerusha's.

BPI has spent many an occasion investigating at the Inn, focusing our attention on the two rooms where Jerusha spent most of her young life, although she has been seen in other areas. Late at night, we have heard the doorknobs rattle, caught the scent of perfume, and one night Laura recorded the gasping sobs of a broken-hearted woman.

Our most active investigation happened on a bitterly cold night in February 2022. We enjoyed dinner in one of their rustic dining rooms, then returned to room nine and spent a few hours perusing the notes placed by guests, asking questions, and attempting to communicate with the resident spirit.

The activity began after 10:00 p.m. We had completed our fourth EVP session and decided to take a short break. Jeanie Foley stepped outside the room to make a phone call, closing the door behind her for the sake of privacy. Room nine has two doorways. The back door leads to the servant's entrance and a stairway down to the first floor. The front door leads to a small sitting room, which then connects to a hallway at the far end. Jeanie stood at the edge of the hallway, within full view of the doorway to room nine and chatted for about six minutes. Inside room nine, we had cameras trained on both doors. Topher Cooper, who had been sitting in an easy chair with his back to the front doorway, suddenly gave a start and remarked that his tri-field meter had jumped to indicate an EMF burst. Simultaneously, we heard the door latch rattle. Bob Pasquale stood up, thinking that Jeanie had locked herself out, stepped to the doorway, turned the latch, and peered out to find Jeanie at the far end of the sitting room, still on her phone. When she came back to the room, we asked if she had closed the door and if anybody had walked past her. She replied that she had certainly closed it on her way out, and that she had not seen a soul. As far as she could tell, she was the only person on the second floor.

Later review of the feed from my infrared camera showed the door latch forcefully turning and the door being pushed slightly inward, yet nobody had entered the room. At the time, we had not seen the footage, so we only had the sudden EMF spike for evidence.

At about 11:30 p.m., I packed up my gear and left for home. Kim Bowman, Bob, and Jeanie had arranged for an overnight stay, taking turns to remain awake and monitor the instruments. At 3:15 a.m., Bob's static field meter lit up on the bureau near the rear entrance, which was recorded on camera. Kim and Jeanie had been lying on the bed at

Jerusha Howe is interred nearby, in Mount Wadsworth Cemetery.

Original, antique furniture graces the first-floor tavern.

3:45 a.m., when Kim heard the door latch rattle again. She sat up and saw the perfect silhouette of a woman in profile, cast as a dark shadow upon the front door. The figure appeared to be talking with a friend, gesturing wildly with her hands, as if she were having an argument. Kim shouted for Bob to aim his camera at the door, but he had been filming the other side of the room, and by the time he swung the camera around, the figure had disappeared. Jeanie had also gotten a quick glimpse of the woman's silhouette. They both described the image as similar to a human shadow cast in sunlight, sharp enough to see definition on the woman's forehead, nose, and jawline. Perhaps they had finally seen the ghost of Jerusha Howe.

BPI will continue to investigate the haunting at the Wayside Inn. We can only speculate that it is poor Jerusha who has remained there for the past 180 years, pining for her lost love. It may be a completely different spirit, or there could be more than one entity. If you ever get to stay in room nine, be sure to leave them a note, especially if you encounter Jerusha!

Some of the verses in Longfellow's haunting poem from *Tales of a Wayside Inn* seem eerily prescient:

> *Round this old-fashioned, quaint abode*
> *Deep silence reigned, save when a gust*
> *Went rushing down the county road,*
> *And skeletons of leaves, and dust,*
> *A moment quickened by its breath,*
> *Shuddered and danced their dance of death,*
> *And through the ancient oaks o'erhead*
> *Mysterious voices moaned and fled.*

Jerusha was an accomplished pianist and often entertained guests at the inn.

Visitors at the Wayside Inn can view an authentic grist mill, still in operation.

11

BETRAYAL AT WESSAGUSSET

The name Wessagusset, in the Algonquian language, translates as "the place where the rocks meet the water."

Having grown up north of Boston, I knew little about Wessagusset Memorial Park in North Weymouth. My friend, Amelia Childs Schwartzman, mentioned it on her popular podcast *Ghosthunting in New England*. Her co-host, Beth Doyle, grew up nearby and would sometimes play there as a child, describing it as a creepy, wooded pathway, littered with brush and dead tree limbs.

To my surprise, Wessagusset was one of the earliest Massachusetts Bay Colonies, established in 1622, only two years after Plymouth had been settled. Why, then, was it not more famous?

And apparently, it is haunted.

For years, the residents on Bicknell Road, which runs parallel to the park, have been frightened by the sound of footsteps, disembodied voices, and ghostly figures appearing within their homes. One resident described seeing the spectral form of a giant Native walk through his living room.

That was enough to pique our interest, so we got a team together on a foggy Sunday evening and headed down to Weymouth, inviting Amelia to join us. We arrived at King's Cove just after darkness, gathered up our gear, and approached the park. We quickly found the entrance on Sea Street. A winding pathway led us into a small, wooded area, and within 30 yards, we felt as if we had entered the forbidden forest. In complete darkness, we waded through grass up to our shins, careful not to stumble over the twisted limbs of fallen trees. I set up a couple of infrared cameras and a REM Pod, and we settled in for an EVP session.

Before we investigate, we usually do a quick dive into the history of the area. The local library is a good source for that, and with a little digging I was able to piece together the incredible story of Wessagusset Colony. The gruesome events that took place here were directly related to Plymouth Colony and some of the most famous figures in American history.

In 1830, Civil War veteran Edward Blanchette was digging out a cellar hole when he discovered the skeletal remains of three headless Natives. He had the bodies reinterred in his own family plot. Two other bodies were later discovered on Ocean Avenue and

Wessagusset Memorial Park runs parallel to Bicknell Road.

Massasoit Road. In 1910, while constructing the foundation for the home of Henry Adams on Bicknell Road, builders Jeremiah Spencer and Waldo Turner unearthed seven more skeletons, buried together in a single tomb. Strangely enough, Adams had five of the skulls inserted into the foundation, where they remain to this day.

While installing a flagpole for the Bicknell Junior High School, workers discovered the remains of a Native woman and her infant child, both with their skulls bashed in. Over the following months, police, forensic experts, and historians went to work and determined that the bodies had lain there for almost 400 years. In March 2008, the town of Weymouth approved a geological study of the area. They used ground-penetrating radar, and it showed that the five Native skulls were still embedded within the foundation wall on Bicknell Road.

Plymouth Colony was established in 1620, their settlement made up of Puritan families seeking religious freedom. When they first arrived, they expected to encounter a hostile land filled with ferocious savages intent upon their destruction. Instead, relations with the Wampanoag tribe were cordial from the very beginning.

Chief Massasoit, a member of the Pokanoket tribe, served as the Great Sachem, a form of spokesman for the four Wampanoag tribes within the area. The Wampanoags, like the Narragansett and Massachusett tribes, were greatly reduced in number at that point. European traders arriving along the eastern seaboard in the 1300s introduced deadly diseases for which the natives had no natural immunity. By the 1600s, it was estimated that the Native Americans had lost 135,000 lives, almost 90 per cent of their population. When Massasoit reached out to the colony at Plymouth, he had been reduced to only thirty warriors and could not afford a confrontation with the settlers.

He sent two braves, Samoset and Tisquantum (better known as Squanto), into the village with a peace offering. Samoset spoke broken English, but Squanto had a good command of the language and greeted the astonished settlers with, "Welcome

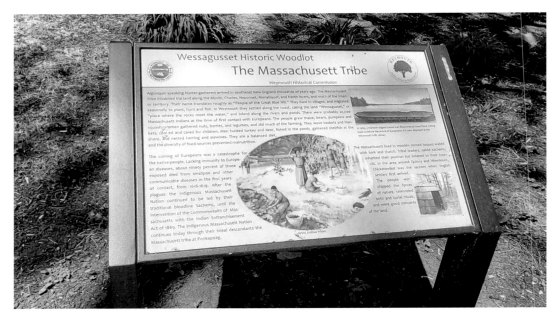

The historical displays describe life in the Massachusett settlement.

Englishmen." In 1614, Squanto had been captured by slavers, brought to England, and then sold into hands of the Spanish. Spanish monks eventually arranged for his release and taught him to speak English. He sailed back to his native land, only to find the Patuxet village gone, devastated by disease. The Wampanoag took in Squanto, and he became a valuable resource for relations between Massasoit and the settlers.

Although the various tribes spoke a common language and often traded with one another, there was a delicate balance of power, based on many factors. When the Pilgrims at Plymouth and the Wampanoag Natives signed that first treaty in September 1621, leading to the holiday we call Thanksgiving, the Narragansett were not mentioned in the document, and likely felt that the balance of power had shifted.

Squanto, at one point, had been kidnapped by a Narragansett rival of Massasoit, who asked the colonists to intervene. Governor Bradford sent his military advisor, Captain Myles Standish, to negotiate Squanto's release. Standish took an overly aggressive approach but managed to return Squanto. This incident was the beginning of hostilities between the various groups.

London merchant Thomas Weston had plans to establish a second colony in the new world, motivated more by profit than religious freedom. He financed an exploratory expedition, determined an appropriate site for the new colony, then followed up with two ships, the *Swan* and the *Charity*, which arrived in Wessagusset in the spring of 1622. The sixty occupants did not come well prepared for life in the new world, their supplies quickly ran out, and when the first winter arrived, they nearly starved to death. Like Plymouth Colony, they survived by trading with the Native Massachusett tribe, led by Chief Wituwamat, who offered them supplies and taught them how to plant corn and beans in trade for blankets, ammunition, and metal utensils.

Myles Standish returns to Plymouth Colony with a gruesome trophy. (*Unknown illustrator, 1874*)

By 1600, the Massachusett Natives were contrived of about 1,000 people living in five settlements: the Saugus, the Cohannet, the Mystic, the Neponset, and the Ponkapoag. Chief Chikatawbak ruled over a nearby village called Moswetusett, and the men from Wessagusset Colony traded labor for supplies, interacted with the villagers, and some even married Native women. Initially, the arrangement was beneficial for both parties, but as the food supply started to diminish, a few of the colonists took to raiding the Massachusett stores.

Chief Chikatawbak repeatedly tried to settle the issues without violence, but their relations became increasingly strained. At the point of starvation, two of the colonists committed an unthinkable act, desecrating the grave of Chikatawbak's mother in the mistaken belief that the Native corn supply was concealed beneath it.

Under threat of reprisal, the colony spent much of their time constructing a palisade instead of farming. Down in Plymouth, the same thing was occurring. As tensions increased between the Wampanoag, the Narragansett, and the Pilgrims, they, too, fortified their village with defensive structures.

The Narragansett, believing that Squanto had been spreading lies among the colonists and claiming the Natives were preparing for war, sent him a personal warning, a bundle of arrows wrapped in a snakeskin. Squanto, however, played it off as a threat to the entire colony, escalating tensions to a boiling point. Captain Standish returned the bundle to the Narragansett leader, filled with gunpowder.

Word got around to Plymouth that the Great Sachem Massasoit was near to death, so Governor Bradford sent Edward Winslow down to Manomet to pay their respects. Instead, Winslow nursed the Wampanoag chieftain back to full health, and out of gratitude, Massasoit informed him that the various tribes were joining forces, planning to attack the two colonies.

Wooded trails wind their way through Wessagusset Park.

Captain Standish had also been to Manomet, trading for supplies and had received a cool reception from the Narragansett Sachem, Canonicus. At their meeting, he encountered two braves from the village near Wessagusset, Wituwamat and Pecksuet, who made a veiled threat to Standish, calling him a "little man" and boasting that Pecksuet was a greater warrior.

The incident that set events in motion involved Phineas Pratt, a Wessagusset colonist who bragged about assaulting a Massachusett woman, then fled the compound, fearing retribution. Two Massachusett braves tracked him for twenty-five miles, but he somehow arrived safely at Plymouth, spouting dire warnings of Native hostilities.

In March 1623, Governor Bradford sent Myles Standish and seven of his men up to Wessagusset, with plans to confront Chief Chikatawbak. Standish invited Wituwamat and Pecksuet inside the compound to share a meal and conduct negotiations. As the meal ended, Standish suddenly stood up, grasped the knife hanging from Pecksuet's neck, and plunged it into his heart. His men made short work of Wituwamat, left the cabin, and rounded up two other Massachusett warriors. They hung one of them inside the palisade, then chased and killed the second.

That was not the end of it, not by a long shot. They went into Chief Chikatawbak's village, killed three of their own colonists, and at least one Native family. Standish then returned to the compound, removed the head of Wituwamat, and taking a white sheet, he soaked it with the blood of the slain warrior. He brought the head down to Plymouth Colony, mounted it on a pike atop their only church, and raised the blood-soaked banner on a separate pole. This gruesome relic became the first flag ever displayed at Plymouth Colony.

With tensions rising and the Native trade falling apart, the Wessagusset Colony was abandoned, and their colonists absorbed into the Maine and Plymouth Colonies. A few settlers remained within the compound, and two years later, they were joined by a group

The Massachusett tribe is memorialized with a Native prayer.

of families led by Reverend Joseph Hull. The settlement finally thrived, was renamed Weymouth in 1635, and incorporated into Massachusetts Bay Colony.

Back in 2021, the area where these tragedies had occurred was now a residential neighborhood. We found a spot roughly 30 yards away from the home containing the five Native skulls. We sat quietly and took turns asking questions, occasionally mentioning some of the names that were involved in the 1622 incident. The K-II meter registered 1.0 mG, and the REM Pod lit up, briefly when we brought up the name, Myles Standish.

As we were about to begin a third EVP session, we heard an odd noise coming out of the woods, a faint trilling sound. We did not give it much thought until we heard it a second time, slightly louder.

Michelle put on her noise-canceling headphones and listened to the SB-7 as it swept through radio frequencies. Unable to hear our questions, she could only repeat what she heard on the Spirit Box. She spouted words that seemed random and unrelated to what we had asked, including "I'm sorry" and the name "Eli." She caught a few more fragments of sentences spoken with an English accent.

The trilling got louder. By now, this animal had become a distraction. The group considered leaving the park.

I said, "I'm sure it's fine. We're pretty safe here. It's so close to the road."

Michelle shouted, "No."

The sound became louder. Whatever this animal wanted, it was coming closer all the time. We could not tell if the spooky sound was coming from up in the trees or somewhere below. We powered up the thermal imaging camera and tried to locate the source. The K-II meter lit up to 1.5 mG.

Tisquantum greets the settlers at Plymouth Colony. (*Unknown illustrator, 1876*)

I asked again if the name Myles Standish meant anything to them.

The REM Pod suddenly lit up like a Christmas tree. I said, "Thank you for letting us know that you're here. Can you back away from the pod?" The unit continued to light up, then started beeping like Morse code. I suspected a battery issue and was leaning down to check it when the sound abruptly stopped.

Michelle said, "Leave."

I replied, "Leave. You want us to leave? This is an opportunity to tell your story. Did something violent happen here?"

Michelle said, "David." The woodland creature called out again, and this time it was right over our heads.

I said, "We're leaving very soon. I'd like to get a little more information. Were you one of the colonists or part of the Massachusett tribe?"

The trilling sound stopped as soon as I mentioned leaving. We asked a few more questions but the Spirit Box had gone quiet. It seemed that whatever entity had been interacting with us had drifted away. We had only been in the park for a couple of hours, but a light drizzle had begun to fall. I was concerned about my cameras, so we decided to pack up and head to the cars. Before leaving, we thanked the spirits at Wessagusset for speaking with us and asked them to forgive us if the park was considered a sacred space for the Massachusett tribe.

Some online research later identified that trilling as a screech owl. Most of the Native American cultures considered the screech owl a sacred animal. Some regarded an owl appearance as the totem spirit of one of their ancestors. Others believed it to be an omen, sent to warn them of impending danger. Animal totems are prominently displayed in Native American carvings and paintings throughout America.

Screech owls are quite often spotted in suburban neighborhoods, but we found it odd for one to approach us so aggressively. Is it possible we had interacted with a totem animal, perhaps the spirit guide for the brutally slaughtered Witawamut or Pecksuet?

In Duxbury, there is a 100-foot monument, topped by a statue of Myles Standish. In the spring of 2022, exactly 400 years after the incident at Wessagusset, a bolt of lightning struck the head of the statue, in effect decapitating Standish in the same manner in which he dispensed Wituwamat.

Pecksuet's gravesite. Wituwamat and Pecksuet's bodies were interred in the North Weymouth Cemetery in 1900. (*Photograph by Cheyanne Wilson*)

12

MURDER AT THE RAMTAIL MILL

How many states list a haunted site in their census reports? The Ramtail Mill in Foster, Rhode Island, is officially listed as such in the 1855 census. The ruins of the old mill are officially haunted.

In a desolate, wooded area near the Ponagansett River, you can find the remains of a small village and the woolen mill factory that sustained it for twelve years. Long abandoned, its only resident is the bitter ghost of Peleg Walker, the night watchman who was brutally murdered in May 1822. At the stroke of midnight, his spectral form continues to make its rounds throughout the ruins, the eerie glow of his lantern clearly visible from miles away. The mill is long gone, burned to the ground in 1873, yet Peleg's lantern floats 20 feet above the foundation, where the second floor once existed.

Local businessman William Potter purchased a parcel of farmland containing an existing grist mill in 1813. He then formed a partnership with his son, Olney, and two sons-in-law, Marvin Round and Peleg Walker, to establish The Foster Woolen Manufacturing Company. They diverted the river by digging trenches and created a man-made waterway, using it to power a massive waterwheel submerged beneath the ground floor of the factory. As production increased, they expanded the site to include a waste house, general store, blacksmiths shop, and five homes for the workers. By 1832, the mill employed twenty-eight mill workers. Ramtail was a common name for wool mills in the nineteenth century. When the woven cloth was stretched out and trimmed, loose pieces fell onto the floor in tiny curls resembling a ram's tail.

Peleg Walker was known to drink and gamble, and soon found himself heavily in debt. His relationship with the Potters gradually deteriorated into a series of heated arguments over money. William tried to alleviate the tension by making him the night watchman while the two Potters managed the business operation. Peleg patrolled the grounds by night, and at sunrise, he would ring a bell that called the mill workers to start their shifts.

On the eve of his death, workers reported a violent argument between Peleg and William, ending with Peleg shouting, "You'll have to take the keys to this mill from a dead man's pocket." When morning broke on May 19, 1822, there was no toll of the bell. The mill workers arrived and found Peleg's body hanging from the bell's rope, the mill keys protruding from his pocket, an apparent suicide. They buried Peleg Walker in a nearby cemetery, and the mill operation soon returned to normal.

Nature has reclaimed the Ramtail Mill.

The footprint of the entire factory is still visible. Even in daylight, the mill is an eerie sight. You can almost feel the eyes of Peleg Walker watching you.

Well, not quite. Three nights later, just after midnight, they heard the peal of the bell. They ran to the mill and found the building empty. For the next few nights, the great bell rang at the stroke of midnight. Now completely spooked, the mill workers removed the rope that activated the bell. That did not stop Peleg; the very next evening, the bell rang at midnight. William had the entire bell removed, and for a couple of nights, they all slept peacefully. One week later, they were awakened by the sound of the mill's machinery. Once again, they arrived to find the mill empty, yet the spindles and looms continued to operate. This went on for days, and occasionally a mill worker would spy Peleg's lantern late at night, moving along the second floor of the building. Mill workers witnessed the great waterwheel rotating in the wrong direction, defying the laws of physics as it turned against the flow of the river.

That was too much for the workers, and one by one, they left the area. Eventually, the little village was completely abandoned, and unable to find mill workers, the Potters had to shut down their operation. The ghost town stood in solitude until 1873, when an arsonist set fire to the mill, perhaps to get rid of the ghost. The fire spread, destroying everything in its wake. Over 150 years, the remains of the Ramtail Mill were reclaimed by the forest. You can access the site with a fifteen-minute hike along the river, where you can explore stone foundations, the housing for the great waterwheel, fieldstone walls, and granite slabs. Much of the area is overgrown with brush, but you can still see the charred remnants of oak beams that collapsed inside the mill.

Peleg Walker's gravesite is nearby, in the Potter family plot. Peleg was often described as an angry and vindictive personality, and he was not well liked. Local historians speculate that he was murdered, and that would certainly explain his need for closure. Paranormal teams have investigated the mill, and some reported seeing the light of Walker's lantern, swaying from side to side as he trudges along the path of his nightly patrol.

The abandoned mill remained silent for fifty years before it burned to the ground in 1873.

In March 2020, Jeanie Foley and I investigated Ramtail Mill during late afternoon. We did not expect to see Peleg's lantern, but we hoped to capture his voice. Although four cameras filmed the area in infrared, we failed to capture Peleg's image, nor did we hear any phantom voices. As dusk fell and the shadows began to lengthen, our Mel-Meter spiked a few times, reading 5.7 mG and then 7.2 mG. Those are extremely high readings for a rural area, but especially so for a site with no electricity.

Peleg Walker is an example of a residual spirit, one that appears at the same time and repeats the same motions night after night without any interaction with the living. Possibly, it is an energy remnant, a portion of his consciousness left behind for eternity. Until we bring in a medium, we can only speculate.

I returned to take more photographs in the spring of 2022. Perhaps because I came alone, the mill exuded a more eerie vibe, and I had the feeling I was being watched. Before leaving, I expressed my sympathy for Peleg's violent death and told him that he has not been forgotten. I sincerely hope that the soul of Peleg Walker will someday find peace.

The charred remnants of the 1873 fire are still visible.

Above left: A man-made waterway flowed beneath the mill and powered the great waterwheel.

Above right: The massive waterwheel was mounted beneath the floor of the main building.

By 1832, the Ramtail Mill housed and employed twenty-eight workers.

13

RESTLESS SPIRITS AT
THE FAIRBANKS HOUSE

Behind St. Paul's Church in Dedham, in the quaint Old Village Cemetery, you will find a number of eighteenth-century burials. Less than 30 feet apart lie the gravesites for eighteen-year-old Elizabeth "Betsey" Fales and twenty-one-year-old Jason Fairbanks. There is a curious inscription on Elizabeth's headstone which reads, "Sainted shade of Heavenly birth, of matchless innocence and worth, Since God decreed you should be slain, We'll cease to mourn, nor dare complain." Betsey was, in fact, murdered in a brutal manner by Jason, her sweetheart at the time, who was tried and convicted of the deed in August 1801.

She had been stabbed eleven times, including once in the back, and left there to die in a pasture owned by the Fairbanks family. Jason then showed up at the doorway to her parents' home, bleeding profusely from self-inflicted wounds, claiming that he had received them while attempting to prevent Betsey's suicide. Poor Betsey was still alive when her parents rushed to the scene but never recovered consciousness, and she died shortly afterward. The Dedham police quickly determined that Jason was their prime suspect, and he was arrested and indicted for the murder.

The sordid trial became a national media sensation, the case prosecuted by Attorney General John Sullivan and defended by Harrison Grey Otis. Within ten hours of deliberation, the jury found Jason guilty, and he was sent to the Dedham lockup to await his execution. However, some local relatives were not convinced that he had committed the crime, and only eight days later, they broke him out of confinement. He fled to Whitehall, NY, where he made plans to cross the canal into Lake Champlain and then travel to Quebec. The authorities offered a $1,000 bounty for Jason's capture. Three Dedham men followed the fugitive's trail to New York, where they came upon him enjoying breakfast in a small cafe, just hours before he had planned to board the boat. The posse turned him over to the local police, and they transferred him to Boston for additional security. On September 10, the day of his execution, two cavalry companies and a volunteer militia escorted the prisoner from Boston to Dedham, where a crowd estimated at 10,000 watched him ascend to the gallows.

As far as we know, that is the only violent incident reported on the grounds of Fairbanks House, a 400-year-old timber-frame dwelling on the corner of East Street and Eastern Avenue. In colonial times, many people died of natural causes within their own homes, so a resident spirit could be any member of the extended Fairbanks family. At one point in its extensive history, the building housed thirteen family members.

Fairbanks House stands alone as the oldest timber-framed structure in America.

The house is filled with colonial-era furniture, tools, and antiques.

Jason was the youngest son of Ebeneezer Fairbanks. Eight generations of the Fairbanks family have graced this historic home. It was built in 1636 and is now considered the oldest known timber-frame structure still standing in the United States. Much of the building was constructed on bedrock, which has helped it to withstand for 390 years. The original frame was built using tongue and groove techniques; there are no nails holding it together.

Jonathan and Grace Fairbanks left England in 1633, settling for a short time in Watertown with their six children. The town of Dedham granted them 12 acres of land and, being a skilled tradesman who earned his living by building spinning wheels, Jonathan erected the main structure with timber imported from England. The spinning wheel business turned a tidy profit, and the family expanded their property in stages, adding a lean-to in the back and a new wing on the east side. When Jonathan died, he left the house to his two sons, Joseph and Benjamin. Ben sold his share and Joseph managed to pass the property down through two more generations of Joseph Fairbanks. By 1755, the house had passed from Joseph III down to Ebeneezer, who made additional improvements, adding a west wing, chimney, privy, and a gambrel roof. Ebeneezer left the home to Ebeneezer, Jr., who passed it down to his three daughters. The last surviving daughter, Nancy, died in 1879, and she left it to her unmarried niece, Rebecca.

Rebecca, the last family member to reside in the home, remained there until 1904, when a bolt of lightning struck and killed her dog. She sold the house to a realtor, but in 1905, the Fairbanks family bought it back again. They had founded a nonprofit, historical organization, The Fairbanks Family in America, in order to preserve the home as a museum. The current caretakers live on the property but in a separate house. The spirits that reside there have never been overly aggressive, or even troublesome. On the contrary, they seem to enjoy the company of visitors. Perhaps it is home to the spirit of innocent, young Betsey Fales.

BPI conducted two investigations at Fairbanks House, roughly eight months apart. The first happened on a rainy November evening, the perfect setting for a ghost story.

The Fairbanks family were among the earliest settlers in Dedham.

Strong winds buffeted its fragile wooden frame, causing shutters to rattle and any number of creaking sounds that could be misinterpreted as supernatural. The children's bedroom on the second floor features an old-fashioned crib, a trundle bed, and various antique toys. It was here that Sara Swanson, one of our sensitives, recorded a clear, Class B category EVP, a male voice whispering, "Oh, my God."

During our investigation, we conducted an Estes Method session using the SB-7 Spirit Box. Kim Bowman served as the sitter, wearing noise-canceling headphones, and reporting any whispered voices that came through the static between radio frequencies. While unable to hear our questions, she offered the name, "Michael." We asked, "Who is Michael?" and forty seconds later Kim said, "husband." Later, during that same session she added, "We are all here." Could this historic dwelling be home to numerous entities?

We recorded strong EMF readings (4.5 mG) on the bed in that same room and 1.5 mG in two other areas. The static field meter also went off three times, with nobody within its vicinity. As we neared the end of the evening, we tried one more EVP session. On the first floor, Kim Bowman and Bob Pasquale both reported feeling deep chills. Suddenly, a strong gust of wind caused the shutters to strike the outside wall, and seconds later we all heard (and recorded) footsteps in an adjoining room. We clearly were not alone.

During our second investigation in July, we caught the haunting sound of a piano. While setting up our gear at the beginning of the night, we left a K-II meter on the counter, next to my REM Pod and Bob Pasquale's static field meter. As we stepped outside to collect more equipment, we looked through the window and saw all three items light up in sequence, as if some mischievous spirit had walked along the wall, passing their hand over our gadgets. Fairbanks House contains only a single electrical outlet, so it is highly unlikely the electromagnetic field would be affected by outdated or faulty wiring.

Later that evening, the Mel-Meter and K-II repeatedly indicated EMF levels in the 1.5–3.2 mG range, and down in the root cellar, where there should have been no electricity at all, the static field meter lit up twice.

None of these things surprised our hosts. They were used to their ghosts dropping by as they conducted tours, held fundraising events, or performed maintenance on the building. On one occasion, the caretaker at the time was setting up for an event in the backyard area. He climbed to the second floor and pulled down the shades of the window overlooking the scene. Behind him, a male voice said, "Leave them open." He turned to find himself alone in the room, chuckled, and opened the shade again, realizing they just wanted to watch the show.

The house has stood for almost 400 years, but it displays some intriguing clues that spirits may have resided there since the beginning. On the first floor above the fireplace, a graphic resembling crisscrossed lines is carved into the wooden timbers and repeated on some of the window frames. Historians describe the symbol as a "hex" sign, and it has been found in many seventeenth-century colonial homes. According to superstition, the hex mark will prevent witches from entering the building. Shoes have also been found, hidden above the ceilings and behind the chimney, another method for trapping evil spirits as they try to enter the home.

The Fairbanks House now serves as a museum. It was declared a National Historic Landmark in 1961 and is listed on the National Register of Historic Places. It would appear that its colonial occupants have become permanent residents.

The caretakers believe that more than one spirit occupies the building.

We recorded a strong EVP in the children's bedroom.

Rebecca Fairbanks, the last of the family, lived there until 1904. (*Photographed in 1920 by Leon H. Abdalian*)

Jonathan Fairbanks established a thriving spinning wheel business.

14

SUICIDE AT THE
JEREMIAH LEE MANSION

On a bitterly cold April night in 1775, three men met covertly in a Lexington tavern, planning their strategy for what would become the first volley in the American Revolution. Samuel Adams, John Hancock, and Colonel Jeremiah Lee were smuggling ammunition supplied by Lee, when their sentry burst through the door with a warning: British troops were approaching Lexington. Barely in time, they slipped out and fled to a nearby cornfield, where they were forced to spend the night huddled against the cold. All three escaped with their lives, but Colonel Lee contracted a fever, which quickly turned into pneumonia. He was brought to Newton and died within weeks. On April 19, 1775, at the Old North Bridge in Concord, the first skirmish took place between the Minutemen militia and British troops. The British charged with mounted bayonets, and the patriots retreated to Lexington Green, where they were joined by reinforcements. The tide of battle turned, and the ragtag rebels forced the British all the way back to Boston. The rest, of course, is history.

Located in historic Marblehead, Massachusetts, is the original three-story mansion built by Colonel Jeremiah Lee in 1768. He only lived there for eight years, but the caretakers are convinced that his spirit never left. Now serving as a museum operated by the Marblehead Historical Society, it is open for public tours. On more than one occasion, the tour was abruptly halted by the sight of a spectral figure—a man in colonial garb pacing the second-floor hallway.

Who was Jeremiah Lee? He was a patriot and one of the most successful and influential figures in the North American colonies. If not for his untimely death, he would have been listed with the founding fathers. According to historical records, he was also a slave owner, housing three in the red brick building behind his mansion. Lee graduated from Harvard in 1768 and married Martha Swett in 1771. He built an empire in the shipping industry, sailing to the West Indies to acquire wine, textiles, fruit, and various commodities, which he sold or traded at numerous ports along the European coast. For twenty-four years, Lee served as a colonel in Marblehead's town militia. Before the Revolutionary War, the colonies had representatives who dealt with the military governors appointed by King George. Marblehead was one of the larger settlements, and Colonel Lee served in that capacity.

As the colonies became more averse to paying taxes to the king, Jeremiah secretly used his contacts in Spain to purchase weapons and ammunition, which were then smuggled

The Jeremiah Lee is a Georgian-style mansion built in 1768.

to various sites north of Boston. According to the tax records in 1771, Colonel Lee, with shares in more than twenty ships, was one of the wealthiest men in Massachusetts. He built himself a lavish Georgian-style mansion with a grand staircase, a banquet hall, a stone facade, and unique, hand-painted wallpaper imported from England, depicting spectacular scenes from current events.

When Jeremiah died in 1775, he had not written a will. To compound issues for Martha and their six children, the American rebellion and subsequent establishment of an entirely new form of government created economic chaos. It took thirteen years to settle his estate, which was finally declared bankrupt in 1788. Martha relinquished her claim to the mansion's title after the death of her eldest son, and Jeremiah Lee's remaining assets were liquidated. The estate passed to creditors and Marblehead Bank purchased the building in 1804. They operated on-site for the next century, utilizing the first floor for banking business and renting out rooms on the upper floors. In 1904, the bank collapsed, and the Lee Mansion was purchased by the Marblehead Historical Society. It was declared a national historical landmark in 1966. Its hand-painted wallpaper is a rare example of eighteenth-century artistry and has gone through a series of careful restorations.

In May 1869, Benjamin Sparhawk, age forty-six, a tenant on the second floor, committed suicide by shooting himself in the chest with a pistol. In 1887, a second bank employee perished at his desk by way of a heart attack.

A daytime tour was canceled in 1992 when a young child saw the ghostly apparition of a young woman standing in the banquet hall. The boy ran out of the building in complete terror.

Above: An apparition was seen in the third-floor hallway.

Right: Jeremiah Lee smuggled guns in 1775 to supply the Minutemen. (*Portrait by John Singleton Copley, 1769*)

In November 2022, the director of programs and operations at the Marblehead Museum invited Boston Paranormal to conduct a full investigation to determine if their building was haunted. We brought along two mediums, Tennie Komar, who is also a spiritualistic minister, and Jacob Abbisso. Tennie strolled into the first floor sitting room and immediately saw a bright orb float across the ceiling. She also felt the presence of Colonel Lee and sensed that he was angry for having lost the estate after his untimely death.

We conducted an EVP session on the first floor sitting room. We had only settled in for a few minutes when we heard an audible whisper come from the center of the room. Our recorders captured it, but we could not decipher the message. Michelle Ross had decided to set up alone in the banquet hall with her Spirit Portal. The portal began streaming through radio frequencies, while she listened with noise-canceling headphones. Since the hall is 60 feet away from the sitting room, with the grand staircase between the two, she could not possibly hear our conversation. Suddenly, the static went silent, and a child's voice whispered to her, "Play with me." Simultaneously, in the sitting room, Jacob felt something poke the back of his head. It appears that one of Jeremiah's six children still roams the mansion.

At 8:45 p.m., we ascended the mahogany staircase and stood on the second-floor landing area, between the bedrooms for Jeremiah and Martha Lee. We had placed REM Pods and motion detectors in various locations throughout the building, and we heard one sound its alarm on the staircase below. Seconds later, the clock chime sounded at

After the Lee estate went bankrupt, Marblehead Bank purchased the mansion, where it operated for a full century.

nearby Abbot Hall to indicate 9:00 p.m., and Laura noted how loud it had been. One of the museum guides lives in a nearby apartment, and she replied, "You should hear that at three o' clock in the morning." The face of Bob Pasquale's cell phone suddenly lit, showing the time. He noticed that it now displayed 3:00 a.m. It is true that our phones can produce odd, little glitches but I would have to consider that more than a coincidence.

A later review of the feed from two separate infrared cameras provided additional evidence. On the third floor, a nursery is decorated with children's toys, and a group of framed oil paintings grace the walls. All these paintings are portraits of deceased children. They had been commissioned in the eighteenth century by grieving parents. One poor child, who had drowned in a nearby pond, was depicted pointing to the spot where he died. My camera had been positioned to face the eastern window, which is protected by a sheet of plexiglass. At 10:22 p.m., the video feed shows the brief reflection of a childlike face turning away from the window, as if she had been peering outward.

We had left a second camera on the first floor in the banquet hall. At roughly 10:40 p.m., while all of us conducted EVP sessions on the third floor, the feed shows a human shadow quickly move across the side of a folding table we had utilized to store our equipment.

All in all, that is quite a bit of evidence for a brief, three-hour investigation. The Lee Mansion is most certainly haunted, and by more than one spirit.

The walls of the second-floor nursery are decorated with portraits of deceased children.

The grand staircase is adorned with rare, hand-painted murals.

Decorative arts from the eighteenth century embellish the second-floor landing.

15

MURDOCK-WHITNEY ESTATE

In 1800, the Morton Converse Company of Winchendon was producing wooden shirt-collar boxes. That all changed one day when the owner needed a birthday present for his seven-year-old daughter. Morton tinkered with one of his collar boxes, combined it with some scrap wood, and made her a tea set. Friends and neighbors began asking him where they could get one for their own children, and he saw the writing on the wall; there was more of a demand for toys than collar boxes. He partnered with Orlando Mason and created a toy-making business that steadily grew into the largest toy manufacturer in the world. Winchendon soon became known as "Toy Town," and the wooden rocking horse was their biggest seller. With the advent of metal toys in the 1930s, the Converse factory closed down. Plastic toys later replaced metal, and those are still produced in Winchendon.

In the center of town stands a 12-foot statue of a rocking horse named Clyde. In 1914, Winchendon turned 150, and the town held a parade. Instead of a float, Morton Converse built a giant, rocking horse mounted on a Model T. The town enjoyed it so much that it was displayed at the tavern, bank, and train station. The current statue is the third generation of Clyde, made of fiberglass because the wooden versions could not withstand the New England winters.

Nineteenth-century wooden toys are on display at the Winchendon Toy Museum, originally housed at the Murdock-Whitney House on Front Street. During your visit, you may encounter more than toys. Museum caretakers often hear the eerie laughter of ghostly children, long after closing time. The mansion was occupied by five generations of families and more than thirty children. It appears that some of them never left.

Constructed in 1850, this Victorian-style classic was the home of Elisha E. Murdock, founder of New England Wooden Ware. The three-story structure features intricate wood carvings, leaded stained-glass windows, mirrored mantles, and a grand staircase. Elisha and Rohanna Murdock had three children, Ellen, Sophia, and George. Little Georgie died at seven, but his mischievous spirit still frequents the mansion. Sophia grew up and married William Whitney, and in 1870, they inherited the estate. Sophia owned a concert grand piano, loved to entertain, and held recitals in the southwest living room. The Whitneys occupied the home through two more generations. In 2000, the estate was donated to the Winchendon Historical Society.

The Murdock-Whitney house, a Colonial Revival with Victorian elements, was constructed in 1850.

Eighteenth-century artifacts grace the Toy Museum housed at the Isaac Morse House.

William Whitney caused a scandal in 1912. For years he had been having a torrid affair, but his young lover suddenly died, and William asked his wife, Adelaide, to raise two illegitimate children. Adelaide was seldom seen in public. She suffered from social anxiety and severe depression and may have mistreated the children. Psychics who visit the mansion are drawn to a room on the third floor they feel is infused with trauma. Those unfortunate children more than likely spent their childhood locked away from the world.

Guests and visitors at the estate report loud knocking sounds, phantom footsteps, and piano music. Caretakers have heard whispered voices and seen full apparitions. The ghostly specters of two different women have been described, believed to be the spirits of Sophia Murdock and Adelaide Whitney. Adelaide gets especially agitated when guests come through her bedroom.

One of the most dramatic pieces of paranormal evidence at the Murdock-Whitney home was captured in 2016 by Spooky Southcoast Radio, using the SLS (structured light sensor) camera system. Invented by Bill Chappell, it uses a Microsoft Xbox Kinect camera designed to map human movement by projecting beams of infrared light. By tracing movement, the software assigns digital points to significant areas of the spectral body, converting the image to a stick figure. Their video (shot with a camcorder) first shows what the human eye perceives, a grand piano sitting unattended in the living room. However, when seen through the screen of the SLS, two stick figures appeared. One sat at the piano, while a second figure stood next to it and seemed to be playing a violin. Both figures moved in rhythm, and the violin player tapped his foot to the tempo. One of their investigators played piano, and he sat down to join the band. When he started playing, the standing figure now held a cello, his right hand working the cords on the neck while his left hand plucked at the strings. Once again, they followed the tempo of the piano player.

Boston Paranormal conducted an investigation on a wintry night in March 2022. By early evening, the snow was beginning to accumulate as I pulled into the circular driveway at the Murdock-Whitney Estate. I was the first to arrive, and after speaking with the caretaker, Ericka, I took the liberty of snapping a series of photographs on each of the three floors. The interior is spectacular, beautifully decorated with Victorian-style antique furniture. As I moved through the various bedrooms and display rooms, I spoke to the spirits, asking for permission to investigate and thanking them for welcoming us into their home.

When Jim, Anthony, and Jacob arrived, Ericka gave us a quick presentation on the estate's history and the paranormal incidents reported over the years. She shared some unusual images captured on her cell phone. One clearly showed a black cat sitting contentedly on the staircase, although no pets were allowed in the museum. A couple of others displayed vaguely human, shadowy figures. Most of the investigators who spent time here had managed to capture compelling evidence.

On his walk-through, Jacob Abbisso, a talented medium, immediately felt the presence of two women on the first floor. In the southwest living room, Jacob sensed an older woman. She seemed very proud of her home and somewhat resentful of visitors. Later that evening, Jacob and I returned to the living room. He suddenly waved his hands in the air, as if fending off a spider's web. "That's exactly what it felt like," he said. "I walked through some kind of webbing but there was nothing there. Maybe it

A perfectly preserved example of a Victorian-style upright piano.

Rocking horses of all shapes and sizes are on display in the Toy Museum.

was electrical energy." I had walked past the same spot only moments earlier and would certainly have noticed a spider's web.

We ascended the grand staircase and set up two infrared cameras on each floor. Jacob and Jim sat in one of the smaller rooms, while Anthony and I settled down on the third floor. Near 9:00 p.m., Jacob's REM Pod lit up a couple of times and the Mel-Meter jumped to 1.2 mG. He then sensed a young child peering around the corner of the doorway. Jacob asked him to come forward, but the child was hesitant. He lingered for a while but eventually drifted away. Jacob later sensed the presence of two men from separate time periods. At 10:15 p.m., an older, bearded man walked across the landing area and into a bedroom. The second visitor was a British soldier in full uniform, except for a black leather shoulder belt crossing on his chest (the British wore white belts to carry their gunpowder).

Anthony had taken several photographs with his cell phone. One of them produced an interesting artifact, the blurred edge of an odd shape peering around the doorway. It somewhat resembled the top of a little boy's head, but could also be seen as a hand, gripping the door frame. On the third floor, Jacob looked out one of the tall windows and saw the reflection a slim, older woman standing behind him. Her energy came across as warm, kindly, and welcoming. He heard a name that began with "S." We determined that he had been greeted by the spirit of Sophia.

We conducted a Spirit Box session in the room where two psychics had encountered negative energy, but it produced very little evidence. By 11:00 p.m., things had quieted down, so we decided to trudge through the snow, cross the street, and investigate a second haunted site. Yes, the Historical Society manages two haunted homes on the same corner.

Colonial mansions (and haunted houses) often feature a grand staircase.

The Isaac Morse House, built in 1790, houses The Winchendon History and Cultural Center. It is also the permanent location for the Toy Museum, where visitors can enjoy a colorful display of antique wooden toys. An adjoining room on the first floor is filled with rocking horses.

Isaac Morse was married twice. He sired ten children with his first wife, Miriam Spofford, and his second, Frances Stephens, bore him five more. Morse, a well-known businessman heavily involved in public affairs, passed away in 1860. The house remained empty until 1939, when it was purchased by Dr. Anton Skelton. Dr. Skelton was also married twice and survived by his second wife, Evangeline, who sold the property to the Porter family in 2007. It is listed on the National Registry of Historic Places.

A building this old must have seen its share of tragedy, but the only documented incident took place in 1972, when a young man used a revolver to take his own life in the basement. We descended to the room where he spent his final moments and conducted an EVP session. None of our gadgets lit up and Jacob sensed nothing unusual. As our time was limited by the impending snowstorm, we quickly moved to the first floor. Three rooms are dedicated to the toy museum, an impressive array of antique marvels that had us completely enthralled. But there was little time for nostalgia and, once again, no attempt at communication by the spirits.

On the second floor, we experienced increased electrical activity. The REM Pods lit up twice, and Jacob sensed the energy of a teenage girl. For almost an hour, the REM Pods blinked in reply to our questions, but we could not get them to light up consistently to indicate a "yes" or "no" answer, which limited our ability to learn anything about the spirit. Finally, Jacob said, "Something has changed. I don't feel her energy anymore." At almost the same time, our gadgets stopped lighting up.

The second floor had certainly been the most active area of the Isaac Morse House, but the snow was piling up outside and we decided to call it a night. Both historic homes deserved a lengthier investigation. We plan to return with a larger team in 2024 and attempt to identify the spirits we encountered.

Young Georgie's shy spirit stood on the second-floor landing and peered around the door frame.

The ornate sitting room where Jacob walked into a "web of energy."

16

GENTLE SPIRITS AT THE PAINE HOUSE MUSEUM

At the corner of Station and Main Streets in Coventry, Rhode Island, stands a three-story, wood-framed colonial home. Currently owned and run by the Western Rhode Island Civic Historical Society, it is an impressive museum portraying life in nineteenth-century America. Original oil paintings line the walls, authentic hand-made quilts cover the beds, and its many rooms are decorated with priceless antiques. The Paine House Museum features spinning wheels, rare books, handwritten diaries, family records, a library, a classroom, and a display room filled with military artifacts from the Revolutionary and Civil Wars.

Although it served as a tavern for more than fifty years, it still projects the warm, inviting ambiance of a family home. Step through the front door, and you will find yourself transported back to a time with no electricity or running water, an outhouse, and a lone fireplace struggling to heat three floors.

Visitors to the museum often feel like they are being watched. They hear whispered voices, tapping sounds, and ghostly footsteps on 300-year-old floorboards. It is unquestionably haunted, but one aspect makes this case unique. An entire deceased family remains there, now believed to be the spirits of William and Sarah Whipple, and their four-year-old daughter, Clara.

The history of Paine House is entwined with that of Coventry. Eighteenth-century town records indicate that Samuel Bennet, who ran a sawmill on the Pawtuxet River in 1691, first erected a single room shack at the site. His son, Samuel, Jr., inherited the property in 1741 and enlarged the building.

Samuel Bennet, Jr. sold it to Frances Brayton in 1742, who converted it to a three-story home. In 1743, the first town meeting and civic election in Coventry was held at the site. Francis passed away in 1783, leaving the house to his son, Francis, Jr.

In 1785, Frances Brayton, Jr. was granted a liquor license, and he then converted the family home into an inn for travelers along the Pawtuxet River. Charles Holden purchased it in 1797, and for almost fifty years, it was called the Holden Tavern. In colonial times, the tavern literally served as the heart of the town. Travelers could spend a night along their journey and townsfolk met to drink, socialize, trade goods, vote, and hear news of the outside world. They also brought their sick and injured for treatment by the only doctor for hundreds of miles. There is a room on the first floor of the museum used solely for medical emergencies in the nineteenth century.

The Paine House Museum was once known as the Holden Tavern.

Museum displays recreate the interior of the tavern as it appeared in 1800.

Charles Holden sold the tavern to Thomas Whipple in April 1849. Phebe Paine and Mary Matteson purchased the tavern in 1866. Mary then sold her share to Phebe and the Paine family held it for eighty-seven more years. The property passed through five generations and finally down to Herbert E. Paine, the last of the family to reside there. Herbert died in 1946, leaving the property to his half-sister, Mrs. Zilpha W. Foster.

In July 1953, Zilpha decided to donate the property to the Western Rhode Island Civic Historical Society as a memorial to her mother, Phebe Paine Johnson, and her sister, Orvilla Paine. The museum was added to National Historic Register in 1974. Many of the antique items that adorn the interior were donated by the Mattesons, Andrews, Tillinghasts, Capwells, and Greene families, whose ancestors had some connection to the inn.

In order to finance the upkeep of these old homes, many of the historical societies partner with paranormal teams who can offer lectures, ghost-hunting tours, and fundraisers. Ken DeCosta is the lead investigator at The Rhode Island Society for the Examination of Unusual Phenomena (RISEUP), which has been conducting research on the museum since 2013. His team has accumulated an array of physical evidence, spent countless hours poring through historical archives, census data, cemetery records, and family journals, to piece together a theory on the spirits who remain at the site.

A little girl has often been sighted at Paine House. She is quite friendly and appears to enjoy having company. Over the years, the RISEUP team has consulted with countless sensitives, mediums, and psychics, seeking to identify the child. Two different mediums came up with the name Sarah, and for a long time Ken assumed that it was the little girl's name. Further research revealed that the child's name was Clara, and her mother

Aside from cooking colonial-era meals, the fireplace supplied minimal heat for all three stories.

The Paine House Museum is filled with eighteenth-century antiques.

was Sarah Whipple, who died in 1866 at the age of nineteen. Only two weeks later, poor little Clara passed away.

Ken and the RISEUP team have developed a unique relationship with the Whipple family. They call the spirits by name, treat them with full respect, always ask permission to bring in guests, and, as a result, have been made to feel welcome in their former home.

Like our Boston team, members of the RISEUP group all come from different backgrounds and educations. They have engineers, medical and linguistic specialists, a psychologist, and even an archaeologist. In recent years, they have developed some creative new techniques for communicating, which has led to a better understanding of the Whipple family and the various spirits that frequent the Paine House.

Many visitors to the museum claim to have caught a glimpse of the child. Although he had been working with the museum for three years, Ken had never actually seen Clara, but that all changed one night in 2013. During one of their paranormal events, a guest had witnessed a pair of legs, floating beneath the dining room table. As you can imagine, that created quite a stir, but nothing further happened for the next couple of hours, so the group moved on to the second floor. Ken used the time to take a quick breather, settling himself in the dining room. Suddenly, the glowing figure of a four-year-old girl floated into the room. She looked straight ahead and seemed unaware of his presence. He watched her move into the hallway and tried to follow, but when he rounded the corner, she had disappeared.

With all his years of experience, Ken was surprised by his strong reaction to the sighting; he was literally stunned and had to step outside to process the event. There is something life-changing about seeing an apparition pass before your eyes. As a parent, his first thought was empathy for the poor child, hoping she was not lost, alone, and frightened.

The museum was once home to the Whipple family, whose spirits remain to this day.

Once the event was completed, they checked the time stamp on their camera feed. They had captured an image of the ghost, but the infrared camera only showed a patch of light travel across the room. Ken saw the figure in sharp detail, yet the camera did not. This is an exceptional observation and would seem to indicate that our individual sensitivity and frame of mind might affect our ability to perceive beyond the veil.

On a chilly November evening in 2018, Boston Paranormal joined the RISEUP team for an investigation at the museum. We set up a couple of cameras on each floor and placed digital recorders in various rooms. Then, we methodically worked our way through each area, asking questions about the Holden, Paine, and Whipple families, and encouraging spirits to engage with us. By the end of the evening, we had come away with some intriguing evidence.

I had left a digital recorder resting on the glass case in the Civil War display room. At 10:15 p.m., Ken slowly walked by, listening through headphones to his own recorder. He stopped suddenly and blurted out, "Whoa! Mark audio!" Then he added, "Barry, you need to check your recorder. I just got a dramatic response, and you probably caught it." Sure enough, when I played my file back, a male voice clearly said, "I'm over here." It remains one of the strongest EVPs we have captured over the years.

Later in the evening, Ken gathered the group together in the dining room for an experiment. He instructed each participant to ask one question, wait ten seconds and then move on to the next person. Once the exercise was completed, we played back our recordings. One of Ken's team had asked, "Clara, are any of your toys here from when you lived here?" In a child's voice, we heard a whispered response, "Yes."

Exploring with the lights out will give you a scare if you encounter one of these mannequins dressed in colonial attire.

We like to experiment because spirits may react only to certain people, they may be afraid of some, or more in tune with others, maybe they can only hear the timbre of a certain voice, or perhaps above or below a certain frequency. You might remind them of their sister, brother, parents, or a friend they knew in life, and that connection could work as a conduit. Investigators sometimes employ trigger objects, such as a toy from the seventeenth century, a familiar antique borrowed from their home, or music from a different era, anything that might stimulate a response.

There are no experts on paranormal phenomena; it is all theory and experimentation. By introducing new and unusual techniques, we may stumble across a better way to engage with the dead. It is possible they are just as eager to interact with the living but are unable to communicate. Perhaps it requires specific atmospheric conditions, or a certain level of energy for them to engage. We are literally stumbling in the dark.

The Paine House Museum can serve as a valuable resource now that they have identified some of its spectral occupants. Initial contact works like a feedback loop, allowing spirits to tell us their stories and encouraging them to keep trying. The RISEUP team appears to have broken through some longstanding barriers, and I cannot wait to hear what else they discover.

Very often, the sounds of a phantom piano have been recorded within the museum.

17

A TRAGIC PLUNGE FROM ASSONET LEDGE

The Freetown State Forest contains more than its share of dark history. Freetown is one of three points that define the "Bridgewater Triangle," a virtual hotbed of paranormal activity that has seen just about every type of phenomenon including ghostly apparitions, floating orbs, Bigfoot, UFOs, pukwudgies, thunder birds, and giant snakes. The triangle, a roughly 200-square-mile area, is defined by Abington in the north, Rehoboth in the lower west, and Freetown in the lower east. It includes Middleborough, Bridgewater, Dighton, Raynham, West Bridgewater, Berkely, Easton, Taunton, and Lakeville. The term was first coined in cryptozoologist Lauren Coleman's 1982 book *Mysterious America*, in which she collected first-person tales and local legends.

Assonet Ledge, a 90-foot cliff in Freetown that overlooks a murky pond, is associated with a Native American tale of forbidden love. As the telling goes, the young daughter of a Wampanoag chieftain fell in love with an English settler, but when their secret was discovered, her enraged father had the Englishman killed. Heartbroken and hopeless, she ran to the ledge and plunged to her death. She now roams the forest in search of her lost love and is often seen standing atop the cliff. It is a romantic tale, but unlikely since the ledge and pond were created by nineteenth-century granite quarrying.

There was an actual suicide at the cliff in 2004; a young man visiting with his girlfriend and two friends inexplicably leaped off the edge as they watched. His family insisted that he had displayed no signs of trouble or depression, which adds to the growing belief that the forest itself was the cause. The Freetown Forest has a well-earned reputation. In 1978, a young, teenage girl was kidnapped, brutally murdered, and her body left tied to a tree. Freetown police found her abandoned bike alongside a pack of cigarettes and a pair of distinctive tire tracks. They matched these clues to local resident James Kater and charged him with the crime, finally achieving a conviction in 1996 after two failed trials.

While investigating the murder, the police uncovered evidence of satanic worship within the forest, including spattered blood, and the mutilated carcasses of young cows. Detectives suspected the rituals were connected to the Fall River cult murders perpetrated in 1979 by Carl Drew and Robin Murphy. There are 50 miles of unpaved roads winding throughout the area, making it an ideal location to dump a body or conceal a crime. Countless physical assaults have been reported along the edges of the

Assonet Ledge is the site of at least one suicide.

Hikers are afforded a spectacular view from the top of the ledge.

woodland. In 1987, a homeless man mistaken for an undercover cop was murdered in the forest, and in 2001, police discovered two bodies on Bell Rock Road riddled with bullets—the earmarks of a mob assassination.

What gives this area such dark energy? Is it the pain and suffering caused by the brutal King Philip's War in 1675? Between the Natives and the settlers, more lives were lost in that one year than during the entire Civil War. For a time, the South Coast area was one giant battlefield. Assonet Ledge is located near a Wampanoag reservation, and Native legends often refer to Pukwudgies (impish wraiths who lure innocent children into danger).

A second theory is based upon geology. There is a high amount of quartz buried throughout the region, a well-known amplifier of electrical energy. Perhaps the abundance of quartz works to attract negative entities and facilitate paranormal activity.

On a clear November day in 2018, we parked in Freetown, hiked half a mile through a grove of pine trees, and found a serene little pond surrounded by a granite shoreline, offering a pleasant view of the graffiti-covered cliff. We climbed up the steep hillside and stepped out onto Assonet Ledge. The view from the top of the cliff is spectacular. We set up our cameras and conducted four EVP sessions. In daylight, the area did not feel particularly creepy, and I had not really expected to come away with paranormal evidence, but I later reviewed the files, and my recorder had captured a woman's voice in a faint whisper, although we could not make out her words. There was a second anomaly caught on camera: a small orb that drifted 3 feet off the ground about 40 feet to our left. It floated into the brush and out of sight.

We never encountered the specter of a Wampanoag princess, but as we hiked back to our cars, I wondered what other dark secrets lay undiscovered within the shadowy depths of the Freetown State Forest.

A steep trail on each side provides access to the edge of the cliff.

Above left: Assonet Ledge rises 90 feet above the pond.

Above right: King Philip was the Christian name taken by Metacomet, son of Massasoit. (*Engraving by Paul Revere, 1772*)

Shot with infrared photography, the landscape takes on an eerie quality.

18

WITCHCRAFT AT THE SALEM LYCEUM

Salem, Massachusetts, is famous worldwide as the site of the Salem Witch Trials in 1692. Commonly known as "The Witch City," it has turned tourism into a profitable industry, with many tours and museums that recreate the tragic events from its Puritan beginnings.

The two-story brick building at 43 Church Street is now the home of Turner's Seafood, a prominent and popular restaurant that began as Turner Fisheries in 1954. Prior to that, it served as Lyceum Hall, a wooden building which burned down in the Great Fire of 1914 and was rebuilt in brick. The Lyceum Bar & Grill operated there from 1989–2011, and Turner's Seafood has occupied the first floor since 2013.

The country's first Lyceum opened in Milbury, Massachusetts, in 1830; its purpose was to provide education and rational entertainment for members of the Lyceum Society. Inspired by the Mechanics Institutes in England, Joshua Holbrook founded the Lyceum Movement in America, and within five years, 100 similar societies sprang up across the country. Their biannual lectures, debates, and dramatic readings encompassed politics, science, the arts, philosophy, and literature.

In 1831, the newly formed Salem Lyceum Society purchased the land at 43 Church Street and erected the red brick building that stands there today. The Lyceums were immensely successful, regularly selling out all their performances, and the Salem location was no exception, hosting such luminaries as John Quincy Adams, Frederick Douglas, Oliver Wendall Holmes, Daniel Webster, James Russell Lowell, Ralph Waldo Emerson, and Henry David Thoreau. You can feel the weight of the building's gravitas from the moment you step through its ornate front door. It was here on February 12, 1877 that Alexander Graham Bell conducted his very first demonstration of the telephone, memorialized by a bronze plaque that hangs above the entrance. Perhaps it is that powerful energy—born of intellectual stimulation—that draws in spirits from the beyond the veil.

Or perhaps it is home to an angry ghost, a woman unfairly accused, tried, and executed during the witchcraft hysteria in 1692. That is the figure most often seen by diners and employees at Turner's Seafood, the ghostly specter of a Puritan woman in a flowing white dress who glares back at them from her reflection in the front window. At times, objects disappear or move around the interior. Picture frames, glasses, and silverware are often flung from their shelves. One employee shared a video clip from their security camera,

Turner's Seafood has occupied the former Salem Lyceum since 2013.

Lyceum Hall in 1900. The hall was rebuilt after the Salem fire in 1914. (*Photo from Frank Cousins' Glass Plate Negatives*)

showing two items literally flying off a display shelf. Two of the current owners, and one former employee, have seen full-bodied apparitions of a woman floating at the top of the central staircase. All this activity drew the attention of two different paranormal TV shows. *Ghost Hunters* and *Ghost Adventures* conducted overnight investigations at Turner's Seafood and came away with some compelling evidence.

The Lyceum was constructed on property formerly owned by Bridget Bishop, one of the most prominent figures from the 1692 Witch Trials. She was the first person hanged for practicing witchcraft. During that tragic period in Salem's history, nineteen people were executed, 200 more victims accused, and one Giles Corey crushed to death by having boulders piled upon his chest.

Bridget was born in Norfolk, England, in 1632. At thirty-two, she married Samuel Wasselby, then emigrated to America in 1660, shortly after Samuel passed away. The young couple had lost two children to smallpox, and their third child died in infancy. Six years later, she married a widower, and they settled in Salem. Thomas Oliver, a local businessman, owned an apple orchard, part of which stood on the future site of the Lyceum. The sweet scent of apples is another phenomenon reported by the staff at Turner's Seafood, some 350 years after Bridget Bishop's death.

Bridget and Thomas had a stormy relationship, and they often fought in public. On more than one occasion, Bridget was seen with a bloodied lip and facial bruises. In 1678, she was called in to court for the crime of disparaging her husband on the Lord's Day, calling him foul names in view of several witnesses. They were both sentenced to a choice between paying a fine or standing for an hour in the public market, gagged, with a note taped to their foreheads that described their transgression. Thomas' son paid off his fine, but poor Bridget was forced to endure this public humiliation.

When Thomas died of an undisclosed illness in 1679, Bridget inherited the house, the orchard, 10 acres of land, and two pigs. Oliver's two sons from a previous marriage received a mere 20 shillings apiece. Only three months after his death, the stepchildren

Bridget Bishop's reflection is often seen in the front windows at Turner's Seafood.

THE WITCH No.1

Depiction of the Salem Witch Trials. (*Illustration by Joseph E. Baker, 1892*)

accused Bridget of bewitching their father to his grave. Once again, their failure to provide evidence allowed the court to exonerate Bridget of the witchcraft charge. But things were changing in Old Salem Village.

It was clear that she was unpopular from the list of petty accusations hurled at Bridget for the next ten years, including stealing brass from a local mill, using foul language, frightening horses, stealing eggs, dressing in a provocative manner, and hosting loud parties where the forbidden game of Shovelboard was being played.

Bridget married again in 1687. Her third husband, Edward Bishop, was a prominent woodcutter and one of the founders of the First Church of Beverly.

In April 1692, Bridget was arrested on the charge of "sundry acts of Witchcraft," accused by five young women: Abigail Williams, Ann Putnam, Jr., Mercy Lewis, Mary Walcott, and Elizabeth Hubbard. While she languished in prison for months, an additional ten witnesses came forward with wild tales of supernatural torment.

Bridget and five other accused women were subjected to humiliating physical examinations that revealed unnatural growths in strange places upon some of their bodies. A second examination concluded that Bridget and Elizabeth Proctor were clear of witch marks.

The trial took place on June 6, 1692, presided over by seven judges, and headed by Deputy Governor William Stoughton. It concluded within a single day. Bridget was not allowed to present a defense, only to answer their aggressive questioning. Adding to the fervor, her five accusers sat in the gallery and went into writhing fits whenever Bridget glanced up at them.

Samuel Grey stated that he awoke one night to see the spectral image of the accused hovering over his infant's crib. The child soon took ill and died. John Louder claimed that Bridget's spectral form would attack him in his bed. He also claimed that she sent a deformed talking monkey into his home to issue threats against him, and that he spotted a jet-black pig roaming her yard. Susannah Gedney stated that she had seen

A bronze plaque memorializes the first public demonstration of Alexander Graham Bell's telephone in 1877.

the same black pig inside her own home, which vanished when she tried to hit it with a stick. Susannah Sheldon testified that Bridget's ghostly spirit confessed to her that she had killed four women. Acting out of self-preservation, Bridget's own husband turned on her, claiming that he heard her speak with the Devil.

The most damning evidence came from two contractors, John and William Bly, whom Bridget had hired seven years prior in order to take down a cellar wall in her former home. They claimed to have discovered poppets hidden within the wall, a form of spellcasting doll made of rags and hog bristles, with headless pins facing outward.

Those accused of witchcraft in Old Salem Village could save their own lives by admitting guilt or accusing others of the same charge; they were released to live the rest of their lives in shame. The Puritans believed that God would mete out their eternal punishment.

On June 8, the jury found Bridget Bishop guilty of witchcraft and sentenced her to death. Two days later, she was taken to Proctor's Ledge on Gallows Hill and hanged in view of a bloodthirsty crowd. As a convicted witch, she was not allowed a burial on consecrated ground, so her body was interred at the execution site.

Bishop was not the first woman accused in 1692, but the judges heard her case quickly because they saw it as an easy conviction. The witch hysteria soon built to a fever pitch, leading to many more convictions and executions before finally abating in 1693.

The mass legislature passed a bill in 1711 that cleared the names of some of the accused witches and granted restitution to their families. It was not until 1957, however, that they officially apologized for the Salem Witch Trials and cleared the names of four additional victims. They amended that apology in 2001, finally adding the names of all remaining convictions.

BPI conducted a cursory investigation at Turner's Seafood in 2023 but came away with very little evidence. We then brought our cameras, recorders, and various gadgets over to Proctor's Ledge, with the same result. Sometimes they are just not in the mood to communicate.

In 2017, a memorial was dedicated at Proctor's Ledge, where a stone marker displays the name of Bridget Bishop. In Salem center, Bridget's name was added to an additional memorial for the victims of the witch trials in 1992. None of this seems to have appeased the persistent phantom that haunts the Lyceum. Nobody can say if their spectral tenant is indeed the unjustly accused Bridget Bishop, but one thing is certain—that tormented spirit will never rest.

Above: Proctor's Ledge is dedicated to the victims who were executed at the site. The inset shows Bridget's inscription.

Left: A warrant issued in 1692 for Bridget Bishop's arrest, signed by Sheriff George Corwin. (*Photo from Frank Cousins' Glass Plate Negatives*)

19

EXECUTION AT SMITH'S CASTLE

The area in Rhode Island known as Narragansett Bay was occupied in the seventeenth century by scattered villages of Native Americans. They called it Cocumscussoc, which in their language means "marshy meadows." The various Narragansett tribes gathered there in summertime to fish and trade.

Roger Williams, a prominent Baptist Theologian, and the eventual founder of the Providence Plantations, came to Cocumscussoc around 1637. He worked hard to learn the Narragansett customs and established peaceful relations with Canonicus, the Sachem of the tribe. Eventually, he purchased a plot of land from the Natives, where he established a successful trading post. Richard Smith arrived in 1651 and purchased the trading post from Williams. The area soon became a nexus for social and political activities, and Smith constructed a large English-style home at the site. When he died in 1666, he left it to his son, Richard Smith, Jr. As the building was heavily fortified against Native attacks, it became known as Smith's Castle.

Within a few years, relations between the colonists at Plymouth Colony and the Wampanoag tribe began to deteriorate. Chief Massasoit, the benefactor who taught the Puritans how to survive the New England winters, had passed away, and his oldest son, Wemsutta, became the Sachem. The Wampanoags were further incensed when Wemsutta died during negotiations with Plymouth Colony. They believed he had been murdered, and when the younger son, Metacomet, assumed leadership of the tribe in 1675, he incited a bloody rebellion that spread throughout much of New England. It was common for Natives to take on Christian names, and Metacomet was known as King Philip. By the end of King Philip's War, twelve colonial towns had burned to the ground and more than 2,500 colonists and an estimated 10,000 Native Americans had been killed. The Narragansett tribe, having been treated fairly by Roger Williams and the Cocumscussoc settlers, tried to walk a fine line by remaining neutral.

The Great Swamp in South Kingstown is a marshy wilderness with its own unique history of paranormal phenomena. In the seventeenth century, the Narragansett tribes gathered there during wintertime. The colonists suspected they had been harboring Wampanoag warriors and decided to attack the compound. The Confederacy of New England, made up of 1,000 soldiers from the Massachusetts Bay, Connecticut, and Plymouth colonies, gathered at Smith's Castle. They marched 12 miles through snow and ice, and on the evening of December 19, 1675, they assaulted the palisade.

Smith's Castle was heavily fortified against Native attack.

The original hearth was constructed in the 1600s.

The Narragansett were massacred, and many of their women and children were forced to flee into the frozen swamp. During the skirmish, colonial troops discovered English settler Joshua Tefft fighting for the Natives. Tefft was captured and brought back to Smith's Castle, where a gruesome fate awaited him. He was quickly convicted of treason, then drawn and quartered. First, they hanged him from a tree until he was close to death, then they split open his stomach, pulled out his internal organs, removed his head, and cut the body into four segments. This is the only recorded incident in American history of a settler being executed in this manner. The colonial militia lost 150 men in the battle, and another forty of the wounded were carried back to Smith's Castle. Only a few survived, and the rest were buried in a mass gravesite.

The Wampanoag retaliated in 1676, attacking and burning down William Smith's home. Two years later, he rebuilt it, adding a stone fireplace, a lean-to-kitchen, and a two-story gabled porch.

Eventually, the Cocumscussoc property was transferred to the Updike, Congdon, and Fox families. In 1692, Lodowick Updike established a 3,000-acre plantation worked by tenant farmers, indentured servants, and slaves. Lodowick died in 1804 and divided his plantation lands among his sons. The farm was bequeathed to Wilkins Updike, including Smith's Castle and the surrounding land. In 1812, Wilkins sold Cocumscussoc to Benjamin Congdon. Congdon struggled to make ends meet and eventually committed suicide in one of the rooms at Smith's Castle. His heirs then sold off most of the property. The house and farm were then purchased by a series of short-term owners.

From 1919 to 1937, the Fox family operated a dairy farm. In 1927, preservationists stabilized the house and performed minor restorations. When the last Fox died in 1937, the dairy farm closed, and the house fell into years of neglect. In 1948, a group of citizens established the Cocumscussoc Association and purchased the property. Smith's Castle was designated a National Historic Landmark in 1993. It is now a museum located in North Kingstown.

So, what kind of activity has been experienced at Smith's Castle? Well, just about everything, including footsteps, doors opening on their own, objects disappearing, disembodied voices, and, many times, a full-bodied apparition dressed in colonial-era attire. It is not surprising for a site that has seen so much pain and violence to display paranormal activity. Besides the wartime trauma, you have also got the weight of some 300 years of slavery and indentured servitude. Infant deaths were common in colonial times, and lives were often cut short by infection, typhus, and smallpox. The staircase alone is responsible for at least one death, a wealthy Newport socialite named Elizabeth Singleton who tumbled down and struck her head. Who knows how many other terrible incidents were never recorded?

In July 2020, I was accompanied by Michelle Ross and Kevin Murphy as we investigated Smith's Castle. The event was hosted by The Paranormal Legend Society of Rhode Island, and we were joined by six other investigators. We agreed to split off into groups and rotate throughout the building to avoid audio contamination. Michelle and I began in the kitchen area, while Kevin explored the surrounding grounds and mass gravesites. The Mel-Meter spiked quite often during the evening. Near the fireplace on the ground floor, it recorded 1.6 mG and, again, in the hallway it rose to 0.8 mG.

Kevin reported hearing the disembodied voice of a child shrieking in the back yard. A later review of audio revealed a young child's voice captured near the exterior wall

Left: A granite obelisk stands at the center of the Great Swamp Fight Memorial.

Below: A lithograph illustrates the assault on the Narragansett compound. (*By John C. Abbott, 1900*)

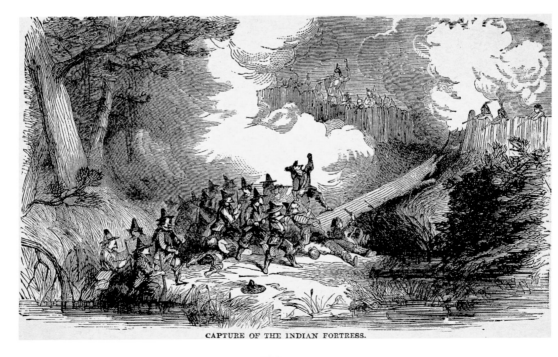

CAPTURE OF THE INDIAN FORTRESS.

of the kitchen. All the windows had been closed, and there are no residential homes within earshot of the castle. Children can also shriek with laughter, but, still, this was a chilling sound.

We swapped off with Kevin and conducted an EVP session near the gravesite for the forty soldiers killed in battle. Our audio recorder picked up a whispered, male voice but we could not make out what was said. In that same file, we later discovered a low growl. As we had been recording outdoors, we could not rule out a wild animal. Our sensitive recorders will pick up sounds from 30 yards away. By now, the mosquitoes were making a feast of us, so we moved back inside and ascended to the second floor.

Before swapping locations with the other group, we listened in on a Spirit Box session they had in progress. As it swept through radio frequencies, they asked a few questions. One woman said, "How old is the building?" and received a reply, "400." Ten minutes went by without another response but then she asked, "How many people are visiting tonight?" and the box spit out, "Fifteen." That seemed wrong until we counted the support staff attached to PLS and realized that the count was accurate. It appears that somebody was keeping track of us.

We spent some time doing an EVP session in the children's bedroom. It was deathly quiet for forty minutes, but then we heard a swishing sound in the display room next to us, which contained a display of spinning wheels. Our recorders picked it up, and we speculated that the door at the far end had opened, but, unfortunately, we had not placed a camera in that area.

Next, we moved up to the third floor and tried a session in one of the smaller bedrooms, with an attached storage area. Michelle heard faint sounds inside the closet, but we could see nothing. Once again, when we reviewed the audio, we found we had captured a child's voice whispering, "Hello."

We climbed up to the attic, which served as the slave quarters. Our EVP sessions produced no evidence, but we both felt a level of heaviness in the area. It was hard to define, but I felt relieved when we descended to the lower floors. Although it was an unpleasant sensation, it did not feel overly aggressive; I would describe it as a profound sadness.

By the end of our investigation, it was clear that the spirits at Smith's Castle are longing to be heard. Perhaps its extensive history of pain and suffering has kept them in a form of stasis, forever reliving the terrible trauma they sustained in life.

The site of The Great Swamp Massacre is memorialized in South Kingstown by a towering granite shaft where the compound once stood. Four stone markers surround it, placed there in 1906 by the Rhode Island Society of Colonial Wars. The plaques are inscribed with the names of colonial commanders, but only one marker pays tribute to the Narragansett tribe that was literally extinguished on a wintry night in 1675.

Above left: The Rhode Island Society of Colonial Wars created a lasting memorial in 1906, but time and weather have ravaged the granite inscriptions.

Above right: A ceremony involving three Native tribes is held annually at the site to ensure that the massacre is never forgotten.

The museum is filled with artifacts portraying colonial life over three centuries.

BIBLIOGRAPHY

Abijah, M. P., *History of the Town of Winchendon* (London: Legare Street Press, October 27, 2022)

Ames, N., *Pirate's Glen and Dungeon Rock* (Boston: Redding & Company, 1853)

Amory, T., *Colonel Jeremiah Lee, Patriot* (London: Legare Street Press, October 27, 2022)

Beauliev, C., "The Fairbanks House: Oldest Known Wood Structure in North America," thehistoricnewenglandproject.com

Bell, J., "Exploring an Old Prison Camp in Massachusetts," newenglandgoodlife.com

Broussard, R., "Celebrating 100 Years at the Palace Theatre," *New Hampshire Magazine*, February 10, 2015 (Manchester, NH), pp. 17-19

Brown, J. R., "Saved from Development, A Place to Dream, Dine," *The Boston Globe*, October 16, 2005 (Boston, MA), pp. 31-32

Citro, J. A., *Dungeon Rock in Lynn Woods Reservation* (NYC, New York: Sterling Publishing Company, 2010)

Clarke, T., *Weymouth: New Chronicles and Old Yarns from the South Shore* (Dover, NH: Arcadia Publishing, October 30, 2009)

Conlon, T., and Bisceglia, D. J., *The History of West Rutland and its People* (Rutland, MA: Thomas Conlon Company, 2009)

Connors, T., "The Bizarre Jason Fairbanks Murder Case of 1801," medfieldhistoricalsociety.org

Daley, L., "Documentary Explores the Supernatural Stories of the Bridgewater Triangle," southcoasttoday.com

D'Agostino, T., "Troubled History Haunts Smith's Castle in Rhode Island," theyankeexpress.com

D'Agastino, T., *Rhode Island's Haunted Ramtail Factory* (Charleston, SC: Arcadia Publishing, September 30, 2014)

Dempsey, J., and Winslow, E., *Good News from New England: and Other Writings on the Killings at Weymouth Colony* (Scituate, MA: Digital Scanning, April 1, 2001)

Eayrs, W. F., *Iron Bars and Genteel Culture in Southeastern Massachusetts: The Development of the Oliver Estate and Ironworks in Middleborough, Massachusetts, 1745–1777* (Boston: Redding & Company, 2002)

Encarnacao, J., "Commission Wants to Preserve House Where Skulls of Early Settlers Found," *The Patriot Ledger*, January 10, 2010 (Quincy, MA), pp. 2-3.

Gravelle, K., "Paine House Puts out the Welcome Mat," *Coventry Courier News*, June 9, 2019 (Coventry, RI), p. 12.

Greaves, G., "Footsteps When No One is There, the Ghostly Laughter of Children. Is America's Oldest House Haunted?" dailymail.co.uk, *The Daily Mail Reporter*, April 14, 2011 (Kensington, London)

Hinkle, J., "Is a Ghost Haunting the Wayside Inn in Sudbury? Two Experts Weigh In," *The Metrowest Daily News*, October 10, 2021 (Framingham, MA), pp. 14-15

Horrocks, A., "The Wayside Inn Ghost: Real or Imagined?" newengland.com

Hoxie, N., "Hauntings on the Assonet Ledge in Freetown State Forest," wizzley.com

Landry, S., "Brothel? Spontaneous Combustion? Debunking Rumors about the S.K. Pierce Mansion," *The Gardner News*, September 22, 2021 (Gardner, MA), p. 11

Landry, S., "Murdock-Whitney and Isaac Morse Houses to Be Investigated in July," *The Gardner News*, July 6, 2023 (Gardner, MA), p. 7.

Lawrence, H. G., *The Coming of the Revolution, 1763–1775* (NYC, New York: Harper Collins Publishing, 1954)

Matteson, G., "The Paine House Museum," westernrihistory.org

Marble, H., *The History of Dungeon Rock* (Boston: Bela Marsh Publishing, 1859), pp. 11-53

McAllister, J., "Salem Tales—The Salem Lyceum Society," Salemweb.com

Mudgel, Z. A., *Witch Hill: A History of Salem Witchcraft* (NYC, New York: Carltan & Lanahan, 1870)

Muise, P., "Ghost of the Assonet Ledge, New England Folklore," newenglandfolklore.blogspot.com

Muse, P., "Weird Marblehead, Part Two: Lee Mansion and Screaming Woman Beach," newenglandfolklore.blogspot.com

Ornell, N., "Floating Frights: The USS *Salem* Transforms into a Haunted Ship," *The Patriot Ledger*, October 16, 2016 (Quincy, MA), pp. 5-6

Raposo, L., "Haunted RI—It's Where History Meets Mystery, Providence," www.ripbs.org

Richards, M., "This Mansion is Big, Old and Beautiful—and It's also Said to be Very haunted," *The Gardner News*, July 30, 2021 (Gardner, MA) pp. 7-8

Robinson, S., "Ghost Ship: History and Mystery on the USS *Salem*," *The Patriot Ledger*, October 5, 2019 (Quincy, MA), pp. 11-12

Savard, R., "Owner Dispels Stories of Ghosts at Groton's Gothic Castle," *The Lowell Sun*, July 14, 2006 (Lowell, MA), p. 21

Schmidt, J., *Fort Warren: New England's Most Historic Civil War Site* (Troy, MI: Unified Business Technologies Press, August 12, 2003)

Segar, D., "The Jeremiah Lee Mansion," StreetsofSalem.com

Snow, E. R., *The Islands of Boston Harbor* (NYC, New York: The Cornwall Press, 1971)

Snow, E. R., *The Romance of Boston Bay* (Dublin, NH: Yankee Publishing, January 1, 1946)

Sweeter, M. F., *The King's Handbook of Boston Harbor* (Cambridge, MA: Applewood Books, 1888)

Tippawong, V., "Visit if You Dare! Murdock-Whitney House," www.visitnorthcentral.com

Toomajanian, C., "Stage Lights and Ghosts: Does the Palace Theatre in Manchester, NH Host Ghosts?" *The Seacoast Current*, October 4, 2022 (Manchester, NH), pp. 15-16

Troost, K., "Paranormal Investigators Host Midnight Visits at Historic Smith's Castle," *The Independent*, June 15, 2018 (Wakefield, RI), p. 9

Trubia, A., "Smith's Castle to Host Paranormal Investigations," *The North Kingstown Standard Times*, June 8, 2019 (Kingstown, RI), p. 18

Tyler, J., *Journey to Middleborough* (Virginia: University of Virginia Press, June 6, 1950)

Upham, C. W., *Salem Witchcraft: Reading the Witch Trials of 1692* (Cambridge, MA: Cambridge University Press, 1995)

Vollmar, J., "Haunted Groton: Indian War Cries," *The Groton Herald*, October 28, 2015 (Groton, MA), p. 7

Walker, L., "Paranormal Activity at the Paine House," www.rhodyradio.org

Winsor, J., *The Memorial History of Boston, 1630–1880, Including Suffolk County* (Boston: James Osgood & Company, 1881)